Praise for *Inside Jobs*

"In an era of sprawling cloud and consumerized IT, the challenge of security is not just to figure out who and what needs to be protected, but how to do so in the simplest way possible. This book drives this point home, and shows how to take friction out of security for users without putting data in jeopardy."

—**Dug Song**, cybersecurity expert, cofounder and CEO of Duo Security, and cofounder of Arbor Networks

"This book addresses a problem that needs focus—insider threat is a very real issue that organizations need to grapple with and understand. It's one of the greatest underserved risks in cybersecurity today."

—**Amit Yoran**, CEO of Tenable, former president of RSA, former national cybersecurity director at DHS, and former director of US-CERT

"I never thought I'd read a book about cybersecurity insider threats that is actually—dare I say it—engaging. By illustrating technical points with compelling stories and examples, this book becomes a productive read not only for the CISO, but also for the CIO, the CHRO and the CEO."

—**Chip Heath**, author of best-sellers *Switch, Made to Stick, Decisive,* and *The Power of Moments*

"Today, some of the most pressing problems in security revolve around insider threats and data security. Code42's new book provides new perspective on these problems and how much more important they have become in the increasingly remote and distributed workplace, suggesting major changes in how we approach data security."

—**Martin Roesch**, cybersecurity expert, creator of Snort, and founder of Sourcefire

"I've seen too many organizations feel they have a cybersecurity program because they have a few cybersecurity products. This book really shows how the care of your data is fundamental to protecting it."

—**Ron Gula**, cyber industry pioneer; developer of Dragon, one of the first commercial network intrusion detection systems; cofounder of Tenable Network Security

"While many executives understand security threats from outside their company, most don't protect their business from insiders. Employees lose, steal, or misplace data more often than businesses realize, costing billions. *Inside Jobs* is packed with powerful examples and actionable advice every senior executive needs to know in a fast-paced book that can be finished in one plane ride."

—**David Meerman Scott**, marketing strategist, entrepreneur, and best-selling author of eleven books, including *Fanocracy* and *The New Rules of Marketing & PR*

"Data leaks are going to happen. Code42's approach to insider threat detection shows you exactly what you need to know when your confidential data is walking out the door and what to do about it."

—**Mike Wasserman,** security orchestration engineer at The Pokémon Company International

INSIDE JOBS

INSIDE JOBS

WHY INSIDER RISK IS THE BIGGEST
CYBER THREAT YOU CAN'T IGNORE

JOE PAYNE, JADEE HANSON,

AND MARK WOJTASIAK

FOREWORD BY GEORGE KURTZ
CO-FOUNDER, PRESIDENT AND CEO OF CROWDSTRIKE

Skyhorse Publishing

Skyhorse Publishing books may be purchased in bulk at special discounts for sales promotion, corporate gifts, fund-raising, or educational purposes. Special editions can also be created to specifications. For details, contact the Special Sales Department, Skyhorse Publishing, 307 West 36th Street, 11th Floor, New York, NY 10018 or info@skyhorsepublishing.com.

Skyhorse® and Skyhorse Publishing® are registered trademarks of Skyhorse Publishing, Inc.®, a Delaware corporation.

Visit our website at www.skyhorsepublishing.com.

10 9 8 7 6 5 4 3 2 1

Library of Congress Cataloging-in-Publication Data is available on file.

The information provided in this book is not, nor is it intended to be, legal advice. You should consult an attorney for advice regarding your individual situation.

Jacket design by Redonk Marketing
Jacket photograph: Getty Images

Print ISBN: 978-1-5107-6448-4
Ebook ISBN: 978-1-5107-6449-1

Printed in the United States of America

Contents

Foreword

George Kurtz

Cyber threats come in many forms. CrowdStrike is best known for stopping threats coming from *outside* your organization: nation-state, eCrime, hacktivism, you name it.

Unlike the global bad actors we track—which our intelligence unit has personified with names like FANCY BEAR, GOTHIC PANDA, and MUMMY SPIDER—insider threats appear in much more benign forms. They can be the friendly network engineer, contract recruiter, or IT analyst whose office is just down the hall (at least it was before the pandemic). In many cases—maybe most—their unwanted actions are inadvertent, or they're simply unaware of doing anything wrong.

When it comes to protecting data, companies need to be vigilant and proactive. And they need systems and tools that let them take immediate action when required. With employees—and outside threat actors—able to work from anywhere, at any hour, with endless options to stash data on devices or in the cloud, every second counts: Incident detection and response needs to happen in real time and without limitations from time zones or geography.

This is precisely why CrowdStrike reinvented end-point and workload protection in the cloud. The effectiveness and rapid adoption of our revolutionary approach has exceeded everyone's expectations—even ours. The same thing has to happen with managing insider threats. Legacy approaches like data loss prevention (DLP) rely on "signatures"—just like the cumbersome antivirus and other end-point systems that CrowdStrike is replacing at enterprises across the globe. These outdated systems are just too complex and cumbersome and can't take advantage of the cloud's speed or scalability the way a cloud-native solution can.

Code42's book comes at an important inflection point for businesses and for the CISOs who keep those organizations safe from internal and external threats. Covid-19 forced companies to redeploy their workers and other resources on a massive global scale, practically overnight. They did it literally to preserve life and ensure business continuity under extreme conditions. Among the many unintended consequences, many organizations suddenly find themselves in a position to experience a huge leap forward in productivity and long-term business resilience, primarily because of moving key systems and processes to the cloud. In many cases, carefully planned business transformation strategies had to be accelerated, and accomplished in weeks instead of years. Some businesses are still reeling from these changes, but are now beginning to see the potential benefits from this forced transformation.

In security, and many other business-critical functions, moving from legacy premise-bound technologies to next-generation, cloud-native platforms has required a leap of faith from the early adopters. Once the benefits become widely known and accepted, truly disruptive cloud platforms like Salesforce, Workday, ServiceNow, CrowdStrike, and others will quickly become the rule, not the exception. As more organizations take that leap—whether from faith or simple necessity—the learning curve for transforming your business with the cloud flattens, and the adoption rate soars.

Today it's easier, faster, and more affordable than ever to provide true and meaningful protection against threats—from outsiders and insiders. This book will provide you with the knowledge and resources you need to make the leap. See you on the other side!

—George Kurtz, cofounder, president, and CEO of CrowdStrike

Introduction

The original title of this book was *The Aha Moment*. As we started working with organizations on the problem of Insider Risk, there were two distinct times in the process when a CISO would lean back in their chair and literally gasp. To be clear, "aha" was not actually the expletive they used, but you get the idea. These moments were visceral, and we started calling them "aha moments," because they became such a regular part of our process of working with new organizations.

The first aha moment happens when we outline the challenges faced when trying to protect an organization from Insider Risk while living in this new world of collaboration and the cloud. "Finally," they say, "someone is addressing this elephant-in-the-room problem." Or, "I knew that there had to be a better way." Or, "This seems so obvious in hindsight, but I haven't had time to consider all these cultural forces at work." What we have attempted to do in this book is to help you get to that first aha moment. It's ten chapters, but it may only take one or two chapters for you to have yours.

The second aha moment is not as pleasant. It's more of a "I can't believe this," or an "Are you kidding me?" moment. It happens when we put in place the technology to mitigate the new threats and the CISO is astounded at *how many* employees are exfiltrating data and *who* are actually doing it. Every CISO and security team knows it's happening. It's the depth and breadth of the problem that surprises most. Junior developers, salespeople, senior execs—they all take data that they shouldn't. If you want to experience the second aha moment, just reach out to us. Since you bought our book and are taking the time to read it to get your first aha moment, we won't charge you to try our product so that you can experience the second one for yourself. We've yet to meet someone who doesn't experience that aha moment.

Thanks again for reading. We hope you enjoy the book and find it helpful.

—Joe, Jadee, and Mark

INSIDE JOBS

CHAPTER 1

The Inside Is Your Blind Side

The potential for data to leak from your organization has never been greater, because taking it has never been easier.
—**Joe Payne, President and CEO, Code42**

"I'm calling the sheriff." That was how he started the call. It was a Saturday afternoon in May and I was in the middle of walking my golden retriever. On the phone was Rick Orloff, my chief security officer. Rick had been the CISO at eBay before he joined Code42, and before that he had been a senior executive at Apple. He was the guy who hunted down that lost iPhone that some engineer left in a bar—it was a big deal, especially to Steve Jobs. Rick had over twenty years of security experience and hung around with people who worked at three-letter agencies. He kept a grenade on the wall behind his desk so when you were on a Zoom call with him, it was always there over his shoulder. "I'm calling the sheriff," he said. "Marianne just downloaded the entire contents of her laptop hard drive onto an external hard drive." Marianne was an employee, but an employee who was leaving our company in five days. This looked like a textbook definition of insider threat.

Marianne didn't seem like someone you needed to worry about. She was in HR, had been with the company for over ten years, and was generally loved by everyone. But when she was successfully spear phished twice in four months, we had to let her go. Spear phishing occurs when a hacker sends an apparently legitimate email to a corporate insider, hoping to get that person to click on a link that installs malware on a corporate network. Because Marianne had been with us ten years, she got a nice severance package and her last day was scheduled for the next week. Everything seemed to be proceeding fine until I got the call from my chief security officer. "I'm calling the sheriff."

Well, as the story goes, we didn't call the sheriff. We called Marianne instead. "We know what you did and when you did it," we told her. "We know the brand and serial number of the external hard drive. Don't touch your laptop or that drive." Her response: "Okay, I just was trying to copy my contacts."

When she brought all the equipment back on Monday, we gave her her contacts. The laptop she had copied had all of our payroll data on it, including every Social Security number of every employee and every board member. It would have been a major breach—an embarrassing moment for a security company. And it was the day that I realized: insider threat is a huge problem. All of our information is portable. All of our employees have laptops. Every employee has some form of critical information. And modern workplace cultures like ours—where data sharing is encouraged—extend trust to employees every day. Calling the sheriff was not the answer. But what was? That's a long answer . . . and the reason this book was born. I hope it helps.

The New Work Reality

Marianne was one part of the collaboration culture that we've built at Code42. She had access to lots of data in the company so she could be efficient and do her job. I know that many of you operate in your businesses the same way. You understand that the success of that collaboration culture hinges on getting the right data to the right team at the right time. That means sharing critical information with all employees, contractors, and freelancers, just like Marianne. To get their jobs done, employees need to crunch, analyze, and organize this critical information in search of the key nuggets that might lead to the next breakthrough. All that data passes through their laptops, tablets, and phones. To collaborate effectively using that data, they need collaboration tools—Google Drive, Slack, Zoom, Dropbox, iCloud, Microsoft OneDrive, and many others.

And what does this collaboration actually look like? I'm thinking about what happens at Code42 in the course of a typical day—probably not that much different than what happens at your company. In the course of a few minutes, you might have Jennifer in legal working on a new customer contract in Google Docs while Andrew in sales shares a presentation with his team via Box. At the same time, Tom in marketing sends me our latest customer research via Slack, while Diane in security uploads a new version of the company security training to Google Drive for employees to access. These isolated moments capture a snapshot in time of the collaborative culture—moments put in motion by ongoing cooperation.

Even five years ago, this type of collaboration wasn't possible. But today it makes us all move faster. Is faster actually better? You bet! And we're not alone in that thinking. To achieve growth rates expected by investors, 80 percent of CEOs, CIOs, and CHROs want corporate cultures to work even more rapidly.[1] This allows us to serve our customers better and get innovation to the market ahead of our competitors. This is the great big upside to collaboration technology. But there is a downside. The downside is that these same technologies that make us more productive also make it much easier to exfiltrate data. The potential for data to leak from your organization has never been greater, because taking it has never been easier. Whether it's an employee like Marianne, who just wants to get some personal information off her work laptop, or a departing employee who wants to give himself a leg up in the job market, your people are exfiltrating critical company information at an alarming rate. According to recent market research, two-thirds of departing employees admitted that they took proprietary data with them when they left their company.[2] In 2018, that translated to 24 million quitters taking unauthorized data with them to their new employers. Of those insider threats, 73 percent went undetected.[3] This book is about how to mitigate that next great risk in security: insider threat.

What Is Insider Threat?

Insider threat is defined as the potential for an insider with authorized access to an organization to use that access either maliciously or unintentionally to act in a way that could negatively affect the organization. From the broadest perspective, insider threat includes any possible inside user action that might cause harm to an organization, such as:[4]

- Fraud
- Intellectual property theft
- Sabotage
- Espionage
- Workplace violence
- Social engineering
- Accidental disclosure
- Accidental loss of equipment or documents
- Disposal of equipment or documents

For the purposes of this book, we're focused on the data loss component of insider threat. Why? Because data loss represents a major blind side for organizations of all sizes. We reframe insider threat as Insider Risk, which surfaces when an employee, contractor, or freelancer moves data outside your organization's authorized collaboration tools, company network, and/or file-sharing platforms.

> **Data loss represents a major blind side for organizations of all sizes.**

The techniques used are surprisingly simple. The most common? While "off-network"—at a coffee shop or at home—an employee uploads an attachment to her web-based Gmail or personal account and sends documents to herself. The second most common type of exfiltration: She uploads files to her personal Google Drive or Dropbox account. The third most common threat is what Marianne did: She downloads files to a thumb drive or an external hard drive. While some of these incidents are caused by frustration or ignorance, like what Marianne did, others stem from malice or a sense of entitlement. Nearly 75 percent of information security decision makers and 71 percent of business decision makers note a pervasive attitude of entitlement among the workforce at their organizations.[5] Many employees believe that if they created something (even if paid to do so), they somehow own it and have a right to keep it when they leave (and they don't). Many even believe that taking company data is essentially harmless.

The case of Jawbone suggests otherwise. Jawbone produced Bluetooth fitness devices. When some Jawbone employees left the company for Fitbit, according to a suit filed by Jawbone against Fitbit, they took really important trade secrets with them.[6] In 2018, several former Jawbone employees

> **Top data exfiltration methods**
>
> • **Personal email**
> • **Personal cloud account**
> • **USB thumb drive**

were charged by federal prosecutors in Northern California with "allegedly absconding with confidential documents when they left the company for rival Fitbit," according to the *Washington Post*.[7] Long story short—Jawbone, valued at $3 billion with 450 employees in 2015, went bust in 2017.[8] That's despite Jawbone lawsuits against Fitbit over trade secrets, some of which Jawbone won.[9] [10] That $3 billion of value evaporated because of an insider threat that wasn't discovered and contained in a timely manner. Insider threat can be a true terminal risk to your organization and its survival.

A New Insider Threat Perspective

How are organizations reacting to this enormous, game-changing new risk posed by insider threat? Well, the data shows that most are not reacting at all. While 89 percent of security decision makers say that protecting sensitive company data is their biggest priority, the same percentage admit it is their biggest challenge.[11] In 2019, 69 percent of breaches involved insiders.[12] And yet, in that same year, only 10 percent of security budgets were focused on internal threats.[13] Sure, we need to protect ourselves from phishing, hackers, ransomware, and viruses. But we need to change the mindset of CISOs to recognize that insider threats are a bigger risk that needs attention. Again, most insider breaches—73 percent—go undetected for months.[14] That means that a Jawbone-like catastrophe could already be occurring in your organization—you just don't know about it yet.

In 2019, 69 percent of breaches involved insiders.

The case of SunPower, a US-based solar energy company, is a good example of the continuous nature of insider threat. In the last few years, SunPower has experienced three major breaches—all by insiders.[15] [16] [17] In these cases, SunPower IP was stolen by employees, managers, and executives through USB drive and email exfiltration. In one of these instances, SunPower sued more than twenty employees and a competitor for trade secret misappropriation, computer fraud, and breach of contract after 14,000 files containing market research, sales road maps, proprietary dealer information, and distribution channel strategies were removed and given to a competitor, according to *pv magazine*.[18] After each breach, SunPower turned to the courts to protect their proprietary technology from competitors, punish competitors and former executives, and win compensatory damages. But relying on the courts is an expensive and slow process. By the time a case gets heard it can be too late—significant damage to your intellectual property and competitive position has already occurred.

We know what you're thinking: "I've got security tools out the wazoo." It's not that your information security department doesn't want to protect your organization. They just need to adjust to the new reality of the collaboration culture. The vast majority of information security professionals rely on blocking access to information to contend with insider threats. Blocking is the literal antithesis of collaboration. Locking down data impedes collaboration and innovation, while actually increasing risk. When technology blocks an action (like sending a coworker a file via Slack) frustrated employees, contractors, and freelancers attempt to evade that blocking with unapproved apps and work-arounds. We see it all the time. The blocked employee simply uses his personal Gmail account or personal Dropbox folder to share the file . . . thus creating even more risk for the organization.

Trying to plug those leaks is a formidable task because they don't occur in isolation. They're infectious. Leaked data is a symptom of a much bigger problem than one frustrated, malicious, or ignorant employee or group of employees. That's because employees tend to share their off-network work-arounds. These work-arounds encourage even more individuals and groups of employees to go rogue in order to accomplish their objectives. Data leaks from rogue insiders put your intellectual property, product development, brand, and reputation at risk. When you fail to contain insider threat, as we saw with Jawbone, the results can be disastrous. What is needed is a change in mindset.

Trust, but Verify

In the early days of network security, we concentrated on building defined perimeters. Once you were on the "inside," we considered you safe and authenticated, and we gave you access to the things you asked for. Today, that approach is no longer considered effective. Organizations are simply too fluid, too distributed, too complex, and too porous. Just because you are inside the firewall does not mean we will give you free rein with corporate assets. We need a similar shift in thinking regarding data loss protection. It is not possible to define policies for all possible actions that may be harmful and then prevent those actions from happening. It is also not possible to classify data effectively across a complex, ever-changing organization.

We need a change in mindset. The new mindset requires us to watch *all* data activity across *all* users and vectors *all* the time. Whether it is source code, sales pipelines, HR data, marketing targets, customer lists, or financial information—it is all important. In today's fluid economy, we don't know which employee or contractor or executive is about to go work for our competitor. The new mindset requires us to trust first, then verify. Because collaboration and sharing are absolutely good for productivity, we trust and we allow sharing. But then we verify the sharing is not high-risk behavior.

> The new security mindset requires us to trust first, then verify.

This mindset shift involves educating everyone in the organization on why security is important and how central it is to the success of the company. Without free access to necessary data, there's no ability to innovate and solve customer problems. But with free access comes the joint responsibility of securing that data. When everyone's responsible for security, an insider breach means that the entire corporate culture—and everyone who is a part of it—is victimized. This mindset turns insider threat into a breach of trust that affects all employees.

Secure the Collaboration Culture

Over the next nine chapters, we'll take you on a journey from the challenges created by the collaboration culture to the solutions that empower it. In the course of that journey, you'll meet our colleagues, customers, and industry leaders who will share their experiences balancing innovation and security.

To that end, this book is divided into three parts:

- Part 1: A New Data Security Mindset
- Part 2: The Change Agents of the Collaboration Culture
- Part 3: How to Secure the Collaboration Culture

In Part 1, we explore the ways in which undeniable business forces, internal cyber risks, and data security dilemmas are pushing the boundaries of traditional security approaches. It's not that traditional security approaches are bad, per se. It's that they can't keep pace with the speed of change within modern enterprises. Massive transformations in workforce dynamics, technology catalysts, and the IP economy are driving the need for new security approaches, which we explore in Chapter 2. These changes place more critical data and information in the hands of insiders, who can put this data at risk all too easily. How? When they use unauthorized apps, work outside your VPN, and use personal cloud and email accounts. And that's just the beginning of the ways that insiders can imperil your proprietary data, as we present in Chapter 3. When you realize how the undeniable forces driving the collaborative culture produce the insider data risks that every organization faces every single day, you'll understand the heart of your data security dilemma. Your organization can't rely on the security approaches of the past, because they aren't equipped to deal with the corporate culture of today. In Chapter 4, we explore the root of that data security dilemma from three perspectives: blocking, the security approach of the past; people, who represent the security productivity challenge; and, finally, technology, which has failed to effectively secure the collaboration culture. We start in Chapter 5 with a view from the top—how CEOs, board members, and the line-of-business managers can facilitate innovation while responding appropriately to insider threat.

Part 2 of the book focuses on the change agents who design solutions for challenges we identify in the first half of the book. Chapter 6 puts the role of the chief information security officers (CISOs) and chief information officers (CIOs) in the spotlight, drawing an in-depth picture of the ways that progressive technology leadership benefits organizations. Chapters 7 and 8 investigate the role of legal departments and human resources in securing the collaborative culture. Then, in Part 3, we offer practical, hands-on frameworks and strategies for security teams that want to launch an insider threat program. Finally, in Chapter 10, we bring it all together and conclude with our best-practice recommendations and view on the future. If you only have time to read one chapter, go straight to Chapter 10.

We started with the story of Marianne, our HR employee who almost created a massive breach by taking all of our payroll data. But she didn't, because we saw the activity when it happened and we were able to get the data back before she left the company. When she was an employee, we never once slowed her down by blocking collaboration. Instead, she did her job in a trusted environment. By only acting when we needed to, we kept the business moving and kept her productive. We understand that this new approach is going to feel strange for security people. It is far easier to sit quietly in a corner and use technology to block possible threats than it is to engage in the messy world of people. Allowing the collaboration culture to thrive means letting people use technologies to share information broadly. It will also mean new engagement policies as we track down those who take data that they should not. We don't recommend calling the sheriff. But you will need to call the employee, and sometimes you will need to call HR and legal, too. We've written this book to help you navigate these new realities in these unusual times. We hope it helps. And we hope you enjoy it.

PART ONE

A New Data Security Mindset

CHAPTER 2

The Birth of the Collaboration Culture

The sweeping change in people, technology, and data that has created the collaboration culture has also created vulnerabilities and risks with traditional data security approaches.
—Mark Wojtasiak, Vice President of Portfolio Strategy and Product Marketing, Code42

It was a Thursday—March 12, 2020, to be exact—at an off-site meeting in Orlando when we made the call: "We're closing the office effective today." They were just six words but they—along with the pandemic—would change how we, and countless other firms, would work together for the foreseeable future.

Those early days of March seem like yesterday—and like a century ago. Originally, the Orlando off-site was an opportunity for the entire Code42 leadership team to get together and talk about our 2020 initiatives. We were looking forward to doing some planning, getting some sun, and maybe playing a little golf.

Then poof! Plans changed. What was intended as a leadership off-site of sixty people centered on success planning became an executive off-site of sixteen centered on crisis response. Covid-19 was starting to spread across the United States, and we could not ignore it. When the World Health Organization says, "We have a pandemic on our hands," you have no choice but to go into crisis-response mode. It was time to take swift action for the health and safety of our employees and business. For two and a half days, we analyzed every aspect of the business through the lens of an emerging global pandemic—business goals, operations, infrastructure, costs, product, and headcount. We ran best-case scenarios and worst-case scenarios. We ran and reran the numbers. We discussed, debated, deliberated, and debated again, and ultimately came to a consensus. We talked about timing, communications, and our message to the company.

To All Code42 Employees:

Our world is changing rapidly. The Covid-19 outbreak is a major health issue for everyone, no matter where you live. It is also a major business issue for Code42 given Covid-19's impact on the economy. I've been meeting with the executive team for the last two plus days to discuss the situation and develop an action plan. This email will attempt to address health and safety issues that affect each of you. I will also address changes we are making in our business plan as we adapt to the changing economy. Thank you for taking the time to carefully read this email in its entirety. Out of an abundance of caution we are making the following changes immediately.

Work from home. We are instituting a work-from-home policy effective immediately for all Code42 employees in all of our offices. Our expectation is that all employees will work from home (or from a safe space, outside the office). We have given much consideration to the pros and cons of this policy. We believe that this is the best policy for employee safety and business continuity. This policy will remain in effect until the public health situation becomes more clear and it is safe to return to congregating at the office. If you need to go to the office to retrieve personal items, your badges will allow you in.

All internal, in-person company events are canceled for the foreseeable future. That includes Mid-Year Kickoff, Experience Week, Sales Club, Succeed42, Lead42, etc. All external marketing and training events also are canceled. This will eliminate the need for anyone from Code42 having to travel for a marketing event.

It will be important to look at your calendar and change any upcoming meetings (both internal and with external vendors, customers, and partners) to video conferences. Our primary concern is the safety of every employee. We believe the above actions are the best options available to us. I have set up a new Slack channel, #ask-joe, where you can reach out to me with questions.

Please stay safe: Wash your hands, maintain social distance, and use your hand sanitizer. We will get through this together.

—Joe

Before the coronavirus pandemic, 25 percent of all US employees, contractors, and freelancers worked from home at least occasionally.[19] In many cases, organizations were able to handle those remote work situations securely because they had ample time to prepare and the specific situations involved acceptable risks to data security. But as the coronavirus spread, organizations were forced to adapt on the fly. Thousands of organizations were forced to implement sweeping changes in a matter of days, sending millions of employees to work from home. To keep employees connected and productive, collaboration software that ran off the corporate network went from a nice-to-have to a must-have—regardless of budgets or cost. That's because in three short months after the pandemic hit, 68 percent of all workers were always (48 percent) or sometimes (20 percent) working from home.[20]

Without a doubt, these sweeping changes related to the pandemic have upped the stakes when it comes to fostering a productive and secure workforce. But the pandemic is not the only market driver behind the evolution in the workforce. In this chapter, we will explore how people, technology, and data have changed and together given rise to the collaboration culture and, ultimately, insider threat.

Collaboration Culture Is Born

What is a collaboration culture? It's quite simple. A collaboration culture is one that actively encourages people to work together. It connects people, technology, and data to drive performance, productivity, results—and ultimately innovation.

> **A collaboration culture is one that actively encourages people to work together. It connects people, technology, and data to drive performance, productivity, results—and ultimately innovation.**

The evolution of the collaboration culture has been taking shape for years. Research by Gartner projected that four in five organizations would change their culture by 2021 as a way to accelerate their digital business strategy.[21] The top enabler of digital business and the reason for sweeping culture change is . . . people.

As 10,000 baby boomers retire each day, their roles are increasingly assumed by Gen X, Gen Y, and Gen Z.[22] By 2030, when the last baby boomers turn sixty-five, the majority of this formerly dominant generation will have retired.[23] Gen X is the new C-level exec; Gen Y is climbing the ranks, if not starting their own businesses; and Gen Z is entering the workforce en masse. Gen Y and Gen Z now make up nearly two-thirds of the global workforce.[24] These generations have grown up not only accustomed to but also believing they're entitled to information sharing—anytime, anywhere, from any device. Frankly, they are the real driving force behind the imperative for sweeping change in corporate culture.

What progressive CEOs have learned is that the corporate cultures of the past are no longer compatible with the younger, more diverse, digital, and mobile worker. Thus, the collaboration culture was born.

The formula to build this new kind of culture is remarkably simple: attract and retain the top talent, arm them with the necessary technology to work together, and broadly enable data access and sharing. Then business results will follow.

> **People + Technology + Data = Collaboration Culture**

According to Deloitte's Global Human Capital Trends 2019, nearly one-third of organizations have already adopted a collaboration culture.[25] And, thus far, over half (53 percent) of those organizations have seen significant results to bottom-line metrics linked to talent, innovation, customer experience, revenue growth, and profits.[26]

Now that we know the basic formula for building the collaboration culture, let's take a look at the historical catalysts that are working behind the scenes to shape each component, starting with people.

People: The Meaning of Work

Finding Purpose

In yesterday's work world, a stable salary and benefits were prime motivators. Workers were more likely to stick with a company—or change jobs if necessary—in pursuit of improved salary and benefits. After forty years of punching a clock, workers were content to retire to the golf course and collect their pensions. Today, the calculus behind work motivation has completely changed. Employees, contractors, and freelancers seek meaningful work over steady work. Across the spectrum of workers, everyone desires more meaning, purpose, a sense of inclusion, and a belief that they can make a difference. People don't choose their employer based on stability and vanity anymore—instead, they prioritize the employee experience.

Employees whose work provides them with a sense of mission and purpose are four times as likely to report loving their jobs than those who lack that sensibility.[27] When the employee experience is meaningful and personal values align with corporate values, 85 percent of workers are likely to recommend their employer to a friend.[28] A sense of belonging is equally important to employees, who want to know that their contributions matter and are recognized. In fact, a survey by human resources firm Work Human reports that frequent recognition builds trust in leadership and creates a buffer against stress.[29] On the other hand, the more stressful the employee experience, the greater the insider threat—a topic we'll explore more in Chapter 8 when we look at the triggers of insider threat across the employee life cycle.

Being Productive

When workers are appreciated and find meaning in their work, their productivity skyrockets. Because they are more self-motivated, they don't need traditional workplaces or work schedules, as we'll explore in this chapter. Maybe the efforts of manage-

Three crucial aspects of the employee experience:

- **Finding purpose**
- **Being productive**
- **Having flexibility and balance**

ment gurus and architects to design and redesign workspaces to maximize productivity are ultimately futile. After all, how fond are you of the open office? How about the cube farm? Perhaps the trick isn't in constructing the perfect work environment or offering the perfect array of snacks and beverages, but in letting people work where they want to work. Plenty of people prefer the predictability and atmosphere of the office. Many others love the flexibility and freedom of working from home, their cabin up north, or, for a change of scenery, the eclectic vibe and caffeinated energy of co-working spaces and coffee shops. It used to be that workspaces were designed to facilitate collaboration, but now that this collaboration is all happening virtually, the focus is changing.

What's weakening the link between work and the workplace is the realization by employees that they don't need a workplace to be productive. Just look at the impact of Covid-19. If anything, we all adjusted to working remotely and most of us figured out how to be productive outside the confines of the office. That's why many don't even care about going to an office—83 percent believe they don't need an office in order to be productive.[30] You know what? They're right.

When the nine-to-five day was created more than a century ago, it was celebrated as an opportunity to provide workers with more leisure time than they'd ever experienced before. The forty-hour workweek arose from a movement to humanize the workplace and provide workers with a respite from physically demanding factory work and manual labor. For decades, this schedule fulfilled its function. But it fails today's knowledge workers, because productivity can't be dictated. Productivity hinges more on the employee's state of mind than the time of day. To that end, only 7 percent of employees believe that they are most productive in the office during regular hours.[31] And if the name of the game is productivity, and employees are demanding more flexibility—then we should give it to them!

Having Flexibility and Balance

How flexible are we becoming? Well, more than half of all workers surveyed by FlexJobs sought to negotiate a flexible work schedule, while nearly one third started looking for a new job in search of a more flexible schedule.[32] Not only do employees desire more flexibility, but they also believe they are more productive and less prone to burnout when they achieve it. And they appear to be right: Employees who are given a choice as to how and when to complete their tasks experience less burnout, according to Gallup.[33] Flexible work schedules present in many ways. Raytheon, an aerospace and defense company, provides an array of flexible work arrangements, including compressed workweeks, flextime, job sharing, reduced hours, and telecommuting.[34] In 2009, Dell launched the Connected Workplace program that promotes part- or full-time remote work. Today, 60 percent of the company's global workforce participate in some type of flexible work arrangement.[35]

For many, flexibility is not only about productivity, but work-life balance. And when work-life gets blended, balance gets harder and harder to find. During the onset of Covid-19, after eight weeks of full-time work from home, boundaries between work and home began to fade. The hours started to blend together. Bloomberg cited some fascinating statistics that paint a picture of the anytime workforce:[36]

- Logging three hours more per day than pre-pandemic work hours
- Starting work later, with peak email time moved from 8 a.m. to 9 a.m.
- Working later overall, as many work as late as midnight to 3 a.m.

The fact of the matter is there's no one flexible schedule that works for everyone. Night owls might go for an 11 a.m. to 8 p.m. schedule, while early birds prefer 6 a.m. to 3 p.m. Others might favor a schedule that shifts depending on the demands of the day—parenting being the biggest factor. The point of offering flexible schedules—just like shifts in the anyone, anywhere workforce—is to empower workers to deliver their best work at their best time.

But, like stress, flexibility also introduces risk. Flexible work hours cloud security baselines for "normal" activity, making it more difficult to spot Insider Risk. When anytime work becomes all-the-time work, and can take place from anywhere, insider threats are even harder to detect. And, let's face it, you can't secure what you can't see.

Technology: Google Docs, Coffee Shops, and Countertops

Now that we've reviewed some of the key historical drivers shaping the people part of the collaboration culture equation, let's explore the technology component. The true enabler of the collaboration culture is technology.

Just as industrialization facilitated mass production, it centralized the globe's workforces in offices and factories. That meant employees of all types commuted into centralized offices in cities and suburbs in New York, London, Hong Kong, and all across the globe. Managers liked that—IT and security professionals loved it. Managers could see what employees were doing and ensure that they remained productive. IT teams could build a self-contained and efficient infrastructure, and security teams could build a rock-solid perimeter to prevent or block sensitive data from leaving the organization. Well, those days are long gone.

The Rise of Cloud Collaboration Technologies

In today's collaboration culture, employees can access the files they need from literally anywhere. Most, if not all, corporate data is now digitized so, with a few keystrokes, it can be accessed and shared by anyone at anytime from anywhere. As part of their daily routines, employees separated by a few feet or thousands of miles can work on the same document concurrently, share data, and workshop a complex problem—all in real time.

To unleash the collaboration culture's promise of creativity and productivity, the number of cloud-based platforms in use has exploded. Almost everything we use today to get our work done is via cloud-based platforms like Slack, Zoom, Google Drive, Box, and Microsoft OneDrive, Office 365, and Teams. Sales has Salesforce. Finance, accounting, and HR have planning tools like Workday and SAP Concur. IT has ticketing systems like ServiceNow and Zendesk. Software developers have GitHub, GitLab, Bitbucket, and Beanstalk. Marketing has Adobe Marketing Cloud,

HubSpot, and the list goes on and on and on. All of this in the name of the employee experience and collaboration, productivity, and speed.

Sidestepping Sanctioned Tools

Most cloud platforms are typically IT-sanctioned. They have passed muster with IT and security and have been rolled out to the organization. However, in the spirit of getting their jobs done, employees often use their personal accounts to access and share company data. At the same time, employees are increasingly relying on unauthorized tools, such as their personal email, WhatsApp, Dropbox, iCloud, and social media platforms to move and share files with team members. In fact, according to the Code42 2020 Data Exposure Report, 37 percent of employees use unauthorized apps daily to get their jobs done. Employees often sidestep sanctioned tools because they believe they are too restrictive and slow—or don't have enough features to accomplish regular tasks. When comparing generational demographics, the younger the employee, the more likely they are to use unsanctioned applications to collaborate. The most commonly used methods workers enlist to move data from one organization to another:[37]

- 38 percent personal email
- 37 percent print
- 35 percent external storage devices
- 31 percent cloud collaboration services
- 26 percent browser uploads

Exfiltration Made Easy

The first three that top the list are tried-and-true methods for sharing and moving data, but the fastest growing are cloud collaboration platforms and web browser uploads. Even five years ago, file-sharing technologies like these, if they existed at all, were far from mainstream. Now, however, they are commonplace, making data even more portable and employees more mobile than ever before. While the tether between employees and their workplaces was gradually loosening, it wasn't until the coronavirus pandemic struck that these employees moved by the millions to remote work. Before the pandemic, nearly one-quarter of the US workforce worked remotely at least occasionally. Between 2005 and 2017, remote work grew by 159 percent.[38]

Yes, technology has made it easy for employees to work anywhere they choose, access any data they need, and legitimately share files any way they want—all in the name of productivity and collaboration. However, technology has also made it easier for them to exfiltrate—or even infiltrate—data like product ideas, source code, and customer lists. The massive influx of cloud-based technology is fraught with risk because data is constantly flowing outside corporate networks. We talked about employee stress as a cause of insider threat. Think about the stressful situation the CIO and CISO now face when it comes to managing and securing the very technology that is being deployed for the sake of collaboration.

All it takes is one employee to intentionally take or accidentally leak data, and an organization could be on the hook for millions of dollars in lost revenue, fines for noncompliance, a loss of intellectual property, and damage to the brand. **This is THE insider threat.** Welcome to the IP economy and the democratization of ideas.

Data: The Democratization of Ideas

Following people and technology, data is the final and third component in the collaborative-culture equation.

Today's varied and ever-changing workforce has a vastly different focus than its predecessors. Instead of manufacturing cars, steel, or widgets, workers harness the power of their intellect for innovation. Of course, innovation isn't new. Since the dawn of human history, people have always sought progress through inventions and production of goods and services. But until the industrial revolution, those inventions and production occurred on a piecemeal and incremental basis.

During the last 350 years, we've experienced three industrial revolutions:

- The first industrial revolution involved harnessing water and steam for mechanized production.[39]
- The second occurred with the invention of electricity, which ushered in the era of mass production.[40]

- The third took it one step further by leveraging electronics and information technology to automate production.[41]

Today, we're knee-deep in the fourth industrial revolution, a digital revolution that is eclipsing the first three in terms of speed, breadth, and depth, according to the World Economic Forum.[42] This digital revolution plays out in many different ways in different verticals. Consider the automobile industry. For decades, the same car companies have manufactured versions of essentially the same cars, trucks, or SUVs. That's Henry Ford's legacy. His genius move at the beginning of the third industrial revolution—the mass production of cars—cut prices, making them available to the mass market. That disruptive move changed modern society. That is, until Elon Musk founded Tesla. Tesla is riding the wave of the fourth industrial revolution, transforming the auto industry with technology. Tesla pioneered or advanced features such as auto pilot technology, auto steering, and the touch screen dashboard, and, with it, automatic updates.[43] Tesla epitomizes the digital revolution through constant innovation, produced by teams of workers who are quickly iterating new products and services. Musk followed the same formula: Recruit and retain top people, give them the technology to be productive, enable access and sharing, provide a sense of purpose (build a car that doesn't spew CO_2 into the environment), and business results will follow. Musk's commitment to the all-electric engine forced other car manufacturers to fast-track production of electric cars. By 2030, 20 percent of all cars will be electric, fueled by billions of dollars of investment.[44]

While the transition into the fourth industrial revolution is a boon for digital companies like Tesla and their workers, the insider threat picture isn't so rosy. The insider threat stakes are high—to the tune of billions. The digital revolution created and is accelerating the democratization of ideas. It's happening across industries, from consulting companies to technology manufacturers and software providers to big pharma, biotech, research, and education. The democratization of ideas is fueling an IP economy and the race for the next big thing. The monopoly on threat no longer belongs to those outside the virtual walls of your organization. It's inside, embedded in the very people, technology, and data that fuel it.

The Culture of Insider Threat—Houston, We Have a Problem

Today's corporate race for ideas has given way to a new collaboration era. We are living in a time when data is being created and shared every second of every day from everywhere. Powered by the latest technologies, employees are emailing, AirDropping, messaging, and Slacking 24/7 from laptops, mobile devices, at customer sites, and in coffee shops. And while these hallmarks of the modern workforce yield critical

The monopoly on threat no longer belongs to those outside the virtual walls of your organization. It's inside, embedded in the very people, technology, and data that fuel it.

innovation, they're also a breeding ground for dangerous data security risks—more specifically insider threats—and CISOs know it. When security leaders are asked what's contributing the most to increasing data security threats, their answer is: "culture."

**"Eighty-nine percent of information security leaders believe the fast-paced cultural model of their business puts their company at greater risk of data security threats."
—Code42 2019 Data Exposure Report**

Houston, we have a problem. We have a disconnect. According to the Code42 2019 Data Exposure Report, 77 percent of information security leaders agree that the most significant risk to an organization is employees doing their jobs however they want, with no regard to data security protocols or rules. In the same report, it's no wonder when asked what was the cause of any data breach in the last eighteen months, half of all information security leaders said internal employee actions—which could mean literally anything from intentional leakage to accidental leakage to incorrect cloud configurations and poor passwords. Needless to say, the risks to corporate data stemming from employees is substantial as 69 percent of organizations say they were breached as a result of an insider threat.[45]

When it comes to insider threat, it's not a matter of if, it's not even a matter of when. Data leakage is literally happening every day. As we've shown, the sweeping change in people, technology, and data that has created the collaboration culture also has created vulnerabilities and risks with traditional data security approaches.

Here's the reality of the collaboration culture. We cannot force people to change the way they work or prevent them from sidestepping sanctioned technology. And we can't lock all data down. So, what's left to do? It starts with detecting unacceptable risk inside the organization and knowing more about the insiders who work there. We are going to introduce you to them in the next chapter.

CHAPTER 3

Insider Risk—A Game of Odds

> When assessing Insider Risk, intent doesn't really factor into the
> equation. Risk is risk regardless of the employee's
> intention—good, bad, or indifferent.
> **—Mark Wojtasiak, Vice President of Portfolio
> Strategy and Product Marketing, Code42**

Many organizations thrive on the collaborative culture, as innovation streams through their ecosystems, yielding breakthrough products and services. However, as we've detailed in the first two chapters, there's a price to pay for the results of all that cooperation—the loss of proprietary information. Unfortunately, this data loss blind spot leads organizations to reject that insider threat is occurring within their companies, thus refusing to take steps to protect against it. There are some organizations that have seen the light—or, shall we say, seen the dark side of collaboration.

Making the leap to concede this unpalatable fact is what we referred to as the "aha moment." It's when organizations understand that data exfiltration can happen at the organization, and, in fact, is happening right now. As we'll demonstrate in this chapter, most Insider Risk stems from workers just doing their jobs in the way the collaborative culture intends. They don't possess malicious intent—instead, they sidestep rules to get their jobs done. Or, maybe they make a mistake because the rules aren't clear—it happens. The fact is the collaboration culture by nature comes with unavoidable Insider Risk. Before we get to exploring why and how employees create Insider Risk, let's start with why Insider Risk is a larger problem to solve than insider threat. Let's look under the hood:

Insider Threat

The very word conjures up images of negativity and malice. Threat tends to center on a specific person or entity and insider threat solutions typically take a user-centric approach. In the security world, threat is often personified by faceless actors in hoodies who seek to deliberately harm an organization. Collectively, there's a reluctance to believe that such sinister characters exist inside our organizations. If they do, they exist at a very minimal level. The reality, however, is that when it comes to securing our collaboration culture, it's not just about malicious users.

Insider Risk

While Insider Risk might sound like a synonym for insider threat, it's not; and there is an important distinction to be made. In fact, we see Insider Risk as a different ball game. When it comes to managing or mitigating Insider Risk, the focus shifts from centering solely on the user to taking a broader, more holistic, and data-centric approach.

Insider threat, as we defined it in Chapter 1, is an event that occurs when an employee, contractor, or freelancer moves data outside your organization's authorized collaboration tools, company network, and/or file-sharing platforms. The focus is on the user—the individual, the person, the employee.

We define Insider Risk, on the other hand, as data exposure events—loss, leak, theft, sabotage, espionage—that jeopardize the well-being of a company and its employees, customers, or partners. Unlike insider threat, which focuses on specific users, Insider Risk, first and foremost, focuses on data.

Insider Risk cannot be viewed in absolute terms. We cannot assume that an employee uploading a file to a personal Google Drive is doing so maliciously—a risk but not a threat. At the same time, we cannot naively assume we don't have employees who intend to harm the organization by leaking financials through a personal email—a risk and a threat. The point is risks can come in shades of gray. In fact, as employees that work for a company, we all personally represent some level of Insider Risk.

Insider Risk is a game of odds, and the stakes are high. As we learned in the previous chapter, the collaboration culture is here to stay. Technology has made it easy for employees to work anytime, from anywhere—a reality that opens up companies to even more risk.

In this chapter, we reveal the many faces of an insider and the risk they pose to the organization. When assessing Insider Risk, intent—good, bad, or indifferent—doesn't really factor into the equation.

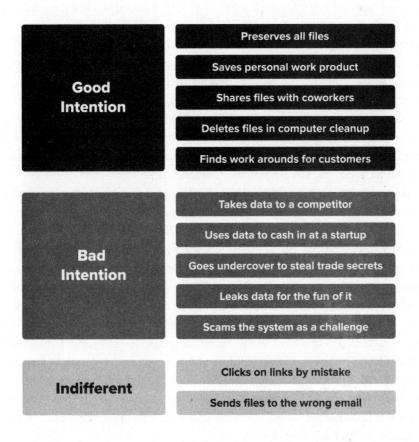

The Good

As organizations become more rooted in collaboration, Insider Risks are inevitable. Why? Because empowering employees to do their best work means giving them access to the tools and data they need to get their jobs done. As we learned in the previous chapter, most employees are well-intentioned, but that doesn't mean well-intentioned behaviors do not cause risk. Employees with good intentions generally assume one of the following Insider Risk personae.

The Saver

This employee typically thinks like this: "I can't stand the thought of losing files, so I save all my files to my personal cloud account. Sure, we have a company policy against this, but the files are too valuable. I just want to make sure they are safe."

Savers' intentions are good. Since when is protecting work product from loss not positive intent? Savers are the most risk-averse people in the organization. They are extremely organized, with elaborate systems for cataloging the files they've accumulated over time. A telltale sign of a Saver is how much storage they use. The challenge with Savers is they don't delete anything, and they tend to automate file syncs to personal cloud services and external hard drives. Herein lies the Insider Risk.

For example, Tom works in product marketing and never lets a good idea go to waste. Tom uses everything from Microsoft PowerPoint and Evernote to Gmail and Slack to capture, organize, and share his ideas. Tom is also an avid Mac user and has his company-issued MacBook set up to sync all of his files to iCloud. That way, he can pull them down and work on them at home on his iMac or iPad Pro. Now, iCloud is not a corporate-sanctioned cloud service, but Tom doesn't care, because as long as he delivers quality work on time, the company benefits. Little does the organization know that since Tom is in product marketing, he has the supersecret product road map on his laptop, and now it's on the loose at home on his iMac and on his personal iCloud. Imagine if Tom worked in Finance or HR. The Saver would have employee records, customer records, and prerelease earnings reports running wild, and you wouldn't even know it. This is just one example of an insider with good intentions.

The Planner

This employee often rationalizes actions like this: "I was just pulling together a portfolio of my best work because I am proud of it. Plus, you never know when work samples may come in handy landing my next big role." Planners should not be confused with Savers. Savers tend to hold on to everything they accumulate. Planners, on the other hand, tend to focus only on the work they've created themselves. If Tom were a Planner, his storage use would be much lower, but the contents of his iCloud could be even more valuable to the organization. He may not have saved the product road map, but he might have the go-to-market strategy he built for the product, and who's to say that file with the go-to-market strategy doesn't contain sensitive information?

The Sharer

A Sharer tends to think like this: "I wanted to provide a colleague my work in progress to ensure the project keeps moving forward." Sharers are often trying to get more coworkers involved in a project. The risk with Sharers is they may send information to people who should not have access to it. What's more, how they share that information could pose significant Insider Risk. What if their preferred method of sharing is a thumb drive, personal email, or some personal productivity web application like Basecamp or Evernote? We ran into this exact situation with an organization. A group of employees loved using their personal Evernote accounts to collaborate. They shared everything from analyst research reports—which incidentally were under NDA so sharing them was a breach of contract—to customer notes, and product strategy and planning docs. All of this living information was being shared outside the organization's sanctioned cloud services and flying under the radar of IT and security.

The Helper

A Helper's actions are influenced by these kinds of thoughts: "I was just deleting files off my laptop to help clean it up for the next user." Helpers are typically preparing to leave the organization. Helpers are sometimes like Marianne—well-meaning employees, yet unaware of the risk they intro-duce to the organization. Let's consider a business case. This employee—let's call her Helen—is leaving her organization on good terms for a step up in her career at another company. Though we are sad to see Helen go, we are excited for her growth and opportunity. Helen was the person everyone sought out for help. Always positive, always getting it done and doing it right. Helen's replacement was starting the next day. To help make the transition as smooth as possible, Helen synced everything from her hard drive to her corporate Google Drive account. We are talking thousands of files uploaded and guess what—all of them shared as open file links. Now Helen worked in R&D, and little did the organization realize, Helen had source code on her laptop. What if the source code is some groundbreaking tech? What if it's the difference between time to market and getting beat to market? We don't know, but what we do know is it's now out on Google for the world to find and see.

The Adviser

Finally, there is the Adviser, whose actions are guided by this type of motive: "I thought my client would benefit from knowing how our other customers structure their contracts." We see Advisers a lot, ironically in services or sales roles. Advisers only want the best for their customers. These well-intentioned employees are some of the best performers at the organization, never giving reason for pause or suspicion and always having a customer-first attitude. Being customer first, advisers want to make things as easy as possible for their customers, and in this case, what may be best for the client is rooted in risk. Consider for instance Ben. Ben is in advisory sales for a consulting firm. Ben has dozens of clients in the biotech industry. Some of his clients use Box to collaborate with vendors and partners. Some use Google Drive. Some use Dropbox. Ben's default collaboration tool is the company's sanctioned Microsoft OneDrive, but Ben cannot allow external access to files living on the corporate cloud, so what does Ben do? Upload files to customers via their collaboration tool of choice. Great for the client, but high risk for Ben's organization. Do the files contain personally identifiable information? Are the files sensitive in nature? Most likely they are, and now they live outside the secure confines of the corporate Microsoft OneDrive account—a situation that is clearly fraught with risk.

The Bad

The malicious insiders—the bad—are the people security teams worry about the most. They come in all shapes and sizes. Their actions create splashy news headlines. Like well-intentioned employees, malicious-minded employees fit into several categories.

The Sellout

This employee just received a very lucrative offer to join a competitor—and not necessarily for their talent, but for their data access. We typically see Sellouts in sales or product roles where access to intellectual property, like customer lists and source code, makes them ripe for poaching. Remember the SunPower story from Chapter 1? SunPower sued more than twenty employees and competitor SunEdison for trade secret misappropriation, computer fraud, and breach of contract after 14,000 files containing market research, sales road maps, proprietary dealer information, and distribution channel strategies were removed and given to a competitor.[46] SunPower's lawsuit alleged that its employees were "solicited and encouraged" to move to competitor SunEdison.[47]

The Startup

This employee is looking for a payday at a smaller, sleeker startup on the verge of making it big. Startups are always on the outlook for IP they can take elsewhere to cash in for stock options or a lucrative executive position, or both. Remember the Jawbone story? Jawbone employees left for Fitbit and took really important trade secrets with them. Although Jawbone attempted to fight back by filing lawsuits alleging trade secret theft, in the end Fitbit won. Jawbone no longer exists. In both the Jawbone case and the SunPower case, the companies turned to the courts. But relying on the courts is an expensive and slow process. By the time a case gets heard, it's probably too late—the damage is done.

The Mole

This worker is an insider for hire—often referred to as corporate espionage. We see Moles most often in technology and telecom, as well as sectors with lucrative research and development programs, like government, higher education, biotech, and big pharma. A recent example of Mole activity is the US government's case against Huawei.[48] According to an article on Quartz, "The U.S. describes alleged efforts by Huawei to steal technical specifications related to Tappy, a robot that Bellevue, Washington-based T-Mobile USA developed for testing phones. The indictment alleges that Huawei's China office directed Huawei engineers working with T-Mobile in the United States to fulfill a contract to supply phones to steal photos, measure the robot, and even steal a part."[49] A US investigation uncovered a bonus program offered to Huawei employees to "steal competitors' secrets."[50] They even had a place where employees could post the information on an internal website.[51] Talk about bold.

Sometimes, malicious insiders come in a combination of forms. The Startup/Sellout/Mole, for example, is a trifecta of insider personae. One of the most notorious examples is the Apple employee who downloaded a treasure trove of Apple autonomous car IP and transferred it to his wife's computer.[52] This all went down in 2018 when he resigned from Apple to move to China to work for XMotors, a Chinese startup that also focuses on autonomous vehicle technology.[53] According to reports, XMotors denied any IP misappropriation and fired the former Apple employee.[54] There are also other types of bad-intentioned insiders who don't make the headlines.

The Prankster

This insider just likes to cause trouble for the fun of it.

The Gamer

This is an employee who is trying to "game the system" to prove that he can.

Perhaps the Prankster and the Gamer are not intentionally meaning to do harm. They're likely just having some fun at the organization's expense. Regardless, the point is that intent doesn't matter if they are creating Insider Risk.

The Indifferent

Indifferent or careless insiders make up a majority of Insider Risks. Their actions are commonly referred to as human error, yet the consequences— the stakes—remain very high.

The Careless Insider

These workers click on links without thinking, accidentally send documents to the wrong email, or just don't realize their actions can be harmful to the company, employees, customers, or partners. Their actions are not driven by intent, but rather out of ignorance, accident, or error. And no one is immune to making mistakes. According to Code42's 2019 Data Exposure Report, 78 percent of CSOs and 65 percent of CEOs admit to clicking on links they shouldn't have.[55] Whoops!

Odds are every organization has careless insiders, and no matter how much security-awareness training you do, you're playing the odds when it comes to securing your data. The stakes? The brand reputation of your company.

Remember Marianne from Chapter 1? She didn't seem like someone who would put our data at risk. She was in HR, had been with the company for more than ten years, and was generally loved by everyone. Before her last day, she copied a trove of sensitive data from her laptop hard drive to an external hard drive—everything from payroll data to the Social Security numbers of every employee and board member. If we hadn't detected the incident in time, it would have been a major breach—an embarrassing moment for a security company. When we confronted Marianne, her response, "I just was trying to copy my contacts."

Every company has a Marianne. Boeing, for example, had an employee who emailed a company spreadsheet to his spouse, asking for help.[56] Little did he know the spreadsheet contained hidden columns with personal information on Boeing coworkers.[57] According to a *Puget Sound Business Journal* article, "The electronic spreadsheet contained 36,000 workers' first and last names, place of birth, employee ID data, and accounting department codes in visible columns.[58] Hidden columns in the spreadsheet also included each employee's precise date of birth and Social Security number."[59] Similar to the Marianne story, this could have been a major breach for Boeing, potentially ending in millions of dollars in fines. To make sure the information never went beyond the spouse's personal email, Boeing had to conduct a forensic examination of the employee's computer and the device belonging to his spouse—and like in the Marianne story—confirm all copies of the file were deleted. Fortunately, the breach was detected and contained.

Another careless insider scenario that made news headlines involves a Prince Edward Island dental practice employee who wanted to prove that they were actually at work.[60] No kidding! Now, we don't know the personal reasons underlying the need for such proof, but we do know that the employee in question emailed a family member a file containing personally identifiable information on over one thousand patients.[61] After investigating, Prince Edward Island's Privacy Commissioner found that the disclosures "were not for any illegal or nefarious purposes, e.g., to facilitate the commission of crimes such as theft, fraud, or harm to property, or to embarrass or harass the clients."[62]

Regardless, the employee's actions resulted in costs—investigative costs, free credit monitoring for patients impacted, public embarrassment, and the potential for future disclosure.[63] Even though written confirmation was provided that "every email and attachment had been 'securely destroyed' and none of the emails had been forwarded to another address," the risk remained.[64] As the company's privacy commissioner points out, "The fact remains that the recipient viewed personal health information, and that the personal health information cannot be unseen by the recipient."[65] And the careless insider's risk lives on.

Insider Risk: The New Normal

Like we said earlier, Insider Risk is a game of odds, and the stakes are high. Technology has made it easy for employees to work anywhere, anytime, on any device.

To ensure your employees stay productive, they can't be obstructed from accessing the very data needed to get their jobs done. To ensure your data is secure, a smart security strategy takes into account a variety of personae and anticipates the malicious as well as the mistakes. That means blocking—and its partner, classifying—are problematic. You can't possibly have the foresight to create a policy for every possible Insider Risk—good, bad, or indifferent. That is the security challenge and, coincidentally, what our next chapter is all about.

CHAPTER 4

The Data Security Dilemma

Today, the very nature of blocking and classifying runs counter to the digitally powered cultures that are built for collaborating and sharing.
—Jadee Hanson, Chief Information Security Officer and Chief Information Officer, Code42

When the security team at a large US big-box retailer decided to block external access to customer credit card information, they were confident they had made the right move. The risks of an inadvertent or malicious leak of this sensitive data were just too high. A few weeks later, the less-than-positive results of this decision were evident. Sure, locking down access to credit card information kept it safe. But it also disrupted an important business function—the flow of late-paying and defaulted brand credit card accounts to the company's external collection agencies.

In response, the retailer's security team had to reassess their decision. To avoid bad debt moving to the company's balance sheet, they had to make an exception to their blocking rule. As it turned out, the collection agencies weren't the only stakeholders that required access to credit card data for legitimate business purposes. By the time a year had passed, the company made hundreds of exceptions to the blocking policy, rendering it essentially toothless.

This case illustrates the difficulties that blocking access to corporate intellectual property can create. What seemed like the best policy—barring access to sensitive data in order to protect it—often impedes key business functions. And because security teams can't possibly anticipate all the potential legitimate business uses for proprietary data, creating exception after exception creates unnecessary additional work for security while making blocking ineffective. It's not only blocking that's in trouble. Classification, another key foundation of current data-protection practices, is also problematic. Why? Because you're asking employees to complete another incredibly difficult, if not impossible, task—to identify, label, and categorize every bit of sensitive company data in order to keep it secure.

The requirements of putting in the right blocking policies and building a sustainable data-classification program leave the security team in a tough spot. These traditional requirements are far from foolproof. In this chapter, we'll explore these problems in more depth to understand why many conventional data security approaches provide little value when it comes to securing collaboration cultures and keeping them productive.

Blocking

The fact is, frequent policy exceptions carved out for legitimate business functions dramatically reduce blocking's effectiveness. Like the retailer example we just highlighted, security teams make exceptions to blocking policies when workers need access to blocked data for legitimate business reasons. We've seen this on the front lines and so have many of our security customers. As soon as you block information, someone—or many someones—will need access to it.

Before we get any deeper into the challenges that blocking creates, let's talk in more depth about exactly what it means to block. Blocking occurs when workers attempt to access or share data or information that they haven't been authorized in advance to obtain or move. In organizations that rely on traditional data loss prevention systems, all data and information is classified based on sensitivity. The number and type of potential interactions between workers and data are staggering. The complicated and ever-changing nature of these systems creates many of the problems that derail security's ability to secure the collaboration culture, as you'll see in this chapter.

There was a time when blocking was an effective strategy. Before the dawn of the collaborative culture and Internet-connected devices, organizations could restrict data to a select few. Today, blocking is incompatible with the collaborative culture. There's no middle ground between locking down information to keep it safe and allowing employees access to the data that fuels today's collaborative workplaces.

Today, blocking is incompatible with the collaborative culture.

Blocking founders on two issues. The first issue is exceptions, which occur regularly when you identify a business process that legitimately needs to be exempt from an existing policy. Exception after exception is documented as part of the blocking policy until your policy looks more like Swiss cheese than an actual effective policy. The second challenge is a complete end run around security protocols so your end users can maintain the productivity levels that are expected of them. Many blocking policies are triggered by content inspection. If content, such as a nine-digit number, is flagged and triggers a block on data sharing, this slows your user down. A nine-digit number could be a Social Security number—or it could be any number used in a document that ends up unintentionally blocking legitimate business processes. In the case of the big-box retailer, a product number is, you guessed it, a nine-digit number. In order for users to get around this, they would put a "0" at the end of the nine digits, easily avoiding the policy block and getting on with their day.

The perils of blocking

- **Always assumes negative intent**
- **Always creates exceptions**
- **Always facilitates work-arounds**

Once data is moved as a result of an exception to a policy or modified based on an existing block, it's off your grid. And without data visibility, there is no way for you to know what users do with it. Perhaps they are collaborating with colleagues on their personal apps for a completely legitimate business purpose. But even if they are, that data is at risk. Maybe they use an unsecured WiFi network at home. Or maybe they will get laid off while working from home and use your proprietary data to find a new job. You may never know.

The reality is employees are willing to break the rules when the rules get in the way of accomplishing their objectives. You might be saying to yourself: "This isn't happening at my organization." But it is—it's just flying under your radar. Just as employees clamor for access to the proprietary data they need to do their jobs, regardless of organizational blocking policies, they resist classification systems—another conventional data-protection tool that's used to reduce the risk of insider threat. We explore that next.

Classifying

Across your organization, your executives, managers, employees, contractors, and freelancers share a common fear. Of what? The relentless drumbeat of security communications prodding them to identify and classify all the information and data that they create, edit, or view on an hour-by-hour basis. Blocking and classification are solutions promoted by many cybersecurity companies to reduce insider threat.

Data and information classification involves two steps:
1. Identifying every single bit of "sensitive" data or information inside your organization
2. Categorizing that data or information by specific levels of sensitivity

Such classification systems are an integral part of conventional data protection solutions. It's easy to see the appeal of such a logical system. However, like blocking, classification systems aren't as workable in practice as they are in theory. In the case of classification, the first issue is that your organization's workers either won't classify or they will classify incorrectly. The second is that classification consumes incredible amounts of time and energy.

Let's look at these problems one by one. Your employees either already are—or will become in the future—highly resistant to classification systems because they:

1. Lack understanding of the rationale behind classification systems and therefore can't properly classify their own work
2. Don't have the time to appropriately classify their work
3. Overestimate or underestimate the importance of their own work, and classify the data incorrectly

Maybe you don't agree with our thesis—that's okay. Let's play out a scenario that we've seen unfold in organization after organization.

The first step in a classification program is asking your employees to go back and classify the work that they've already produced. Most workers have hundreds—if not thousands—of work projects, documents, and pieces of information pass through their hands. Based on the new process, they need to reread them, understand what they mean, and consider where in the security classification they should fall. To have to go back and classify everything takes a lot of time that potentially pulls them away from their regular work assignments.

If they do manage to get a grip on all of their historical data and information, they then have to shoulder double duty with all of their current workload. That means doing their actual work and then classifying their actual work. We've seen how every worker's days relentlessly fill up with classification responsibilities to the point where classification takes over. As this happens across your organization, less and less actual work gets done. Business priorities get squeezed by an unending cycle of classification tasks.

The gap between business needs and security needs widens further as security continues to push the doomed classification initiative. The dream of a bulletproof security classification system implodes into a nightmare. Instead of an actual functioning insider threat security system, there's a nonfunctional classification system that everyone ignores. It doesn't work—but it exists on paper.

There's usually a point at which security teams acknowledge the reality—at least internally. How do we know? We've worked at organizations that zealously enforced classification policies. What the top brass didn't know was that the security team itself ignored the classification policy to the point of issuing security briefings that weren't themselves classified.

> **Like blocking, classification systems come from a rational perspective. However, the rational perspective is rooted in the past, in a work culture that doesn't exist anymore.**

Like blocking, classification systems come from a rational perspective. However, the rational perspective is rooted in the past, in a work culture that doesn't exist anymore. Classification systems had a chance in the past because data was easier to locate and lock down to a device or server. With collaboration and the cloud, this is no longer the case, especially for user-created content like source code, strategy documents, and customer lists. Plus, collaboration did not happen at the same real-time pace we see across modern workforces. Today, the very nature of blocking and classifying runs counter to the digitally powered cultures that are being built for collaborating and sharing. It doesn't mean blocking and classifying are bad—they just no longer provide the level of protection your proprietary user-generated data needs.

Tools such as blocking and classification, when they don't work, contribute to an all-too-often unacknowledged problem in corporate cultures—the insidious gap between policy and practice. That's up next.

Gap Between Policy and Practice

Many organizations try to embrace a collaborative culture without shifting away from conventional security norms. This sends mixed messages to employees, contractors, and freelancers, creating an obvious gap between policy and practice. This can come back to bite you in two ways, by:

- Setting up conflict between achieving work and security goals
- Opening the door to security breaches that compromise intellectual property

It's never a good idea to put your employees in a situation where they have to choose between conflicting priorities, such as keeping their bosses happy or adhering to company security policy. Still, we know who wins in this situation, don't we? Bosses—every time! Today's fast-moving corporate culture places the burden on the employee to meet their bosses' objectives. Workers understand that leaders are looking for productivity and profitability. Inevitably, that means security protocols get overlooked because the price of not meeting deadlines is higher in the short run than any potential blowback from security.

This situation leads to security work-arounds. There are many other potential ways that inconvenience and frustration can cause end runs around security policy. Perhaps a contractor needs access to proprietary information, so instead of requesting a new user ID and password through proper channels, an employee shares their log-in and password. In fact, more than one-third of employees were willing to share sensitive data if that data helped them or others do their job more effectively, according to a 2017 study.[66]

> **The potential danger in the gap between policy and practice is that it creates an *illusion* of protection from insider threats.**

The potential danger in the gap between policy and practice is that it creates an *illusion* of protection from insider threats. Security leaders and the c-suite may feel confident that their robust security program will protect them from insider threat. This misplaced faith blinds organizations to how vulnerable they are, sidetracks them from evaluating alternative insider threat solutions, and ties up their budget in tech that doesn't solve their problems.

Cost of Outdated Solutions

The gap between process and practice also creates another potential problem. Security breaches are expensive and embarrassing. While the cost of insider threat incidents varies based on the cause, the end result isn't pretty no matter how it happens:[67]

- Negligent insiders: $307,111 per incident
- Thief stealing insider credentials: $871,686 per incident
- Malicious insiders: $755,760 per incident

Insider threats increased by 47 percent from 2018 to 2020.

If conventional approaches such as blocking and classification worked as an insider threat deterrent, insider threat wouldn't be such a big issue. But it is an expensive and growing problem. Insider threats increased by 47 percent from 2018 to 2020.[68] Not only are there more threats, but the incidents that occur are also more costly—rising from $8.76 million in 2018 to $11.45 million in 2020.[69] As much as we all wish that traditional approaches worked, they don't.

When you examine the problematic implications of blocking and classification, you can see they not only fail as a data security approach, they also carry hefty financial consequences. That's because they soak up 90 percent of your organization's data-protection budget.[70] During these uncertain economic times, it's especially difficult to stomach spending so much money on ineffective solutions.

Security Productivity

Not only can conventional blocking and classification systems encourage security work-arounds and come with financial challenges, they also create productivity issues. This applies to all aspects of business—from the marketing manager who is trying to access customer data to finish an executive report to the security analyst in charge of data loss prevention (DLP).

Meet Trey. He's a mid-level security analyst at a division of a food-service company. Trey works with the DLP system that his division just implemented. It's Trey's job to ensure division employees appropriately classify and label data. Data that meets specific sensitivity criteria is blocked to prevent a compromise to data security. Like his security colleagues in other security departments, Trey is constantly wrestling with an out-of-control data-classification system.

Not only does he have trouble getting his colleagues to classify their work, but he also keeps finding more data that requires classification. His classification project keeps ballooning in size and complexity, pushing deliverables and deadlines further into the future.

After six more months of fruitless efforts to build a sustainable system, Trey—and his boss—throw in the towel. They turn their data loss policies off and put the DLP system in monitor-only mode. Turning blocking off has created a vicious cycle of guesswork and doubt. Trey knows that much of the data is either not classified at all or is over- or under-classified. He finally understands that the system that he and his colleagues have bought into, emotionally and financially, is broken. He sees the future—days, nights, and weekends chasing the false alerts that the system throws off.

To plug the holes, Trey's company, like other organizations, often decides to invest in more tech, such as User Behavior Analytics (UBA), User and Entity Behavior Analytics (UEBA), or User Activity Monitoring (UAM). That way, the security team can surveil employees to collect user behavior designed to spot insider threats to sensitive data. Instead of focusing on work product, you focus on users.

And so Trey gets pulled into another security strategy—except, it's essentially the same song, different tune. This time he is tasked with identifying all of the users in the organization with access to sensitive data. He creates a baseline for "normal" versus "abnormal" user behavior, and then crafts a policy or rule that kicks off an alert when users behave abnormally.

Guess what happens? Those darned alerts just keep coming, and Trey is caught in another endless cycle of tasks. This time he's defining and redefining baselines in an effort to avoid having to chase down so many false positives.

Instead of defining policies for what data is sensitive or not sensitive, this time Trey is creating policies for what is normal versus abnormal user behavior. Once again, how could Trey, or any security team for that matter, possibly have the foresight to make that determination? It was hard enough to assess routine behavior while everyone was in a centralized corporate office. Good luck now that everyone is working from home. What was "unusual" yesterday is "normal" today. And what is normal today may not be the standard tomorrow. It depends on the user and the day. Just try to keep up with that.

Perhaps the solution is smarter tech in the form of artificial intelligence (AI) and machine learning (ML). These technologies are being touted by some as the solutions needed to ease the pain of the security practitioner. Wouldn't we all love to actually let the machine do the work for a change? But here's the rub—you still have to teach the machine what to do. Once again, the success of the tech is dependent on the security team and their collective foresight.

> **It's time for all of us to realize that the old conventional ways of protecting data are no longer enough to secure today's fast-paced collaborative cultures.**

Bottom line? It's time for all of us to realize that the old conventional ways of protecting data are no longer enough to secure today's fast-paced collaborative cultures. They've failed to keep pace with the way people work. They're complex, laborious, and expensive. Traditional policy-based security approaches were designed to focus on compliance and protecting PII, PCI, and PHI, not IP. But in today's world, where corporate futures rely on the speed of innovation, ideas and IP are equally as important. To meet these new expectations—while addressing Insider Risk more holistically—we've got to adopt new data protection methods that actually set the security practitioner up for success and work without slowing down company productivity.

Where We Go From Here

Making the shift in our approach to data security does not start with amazing new tech. Instead, it starts with a change in attitude. Instead of assuming workers are trying to get away with something—negative intent—presume that they mean well and are just trying to get their jobs done in the best way they know how. We call that positive intent. It might not sound like a game changer, but it is. When you and your security team presume that employees are trying to do the right thing instead of the wrong thing, it's much easier for the business and information security to act as the allies they should be rather than adversaries.

When organizations embed positive intent throughout their departments and divisions and transform security from policing to partnering, there's a much better chance to contain Insider Risk. In Part 2 of this book, we'll show you how you can adopt practices that bake security into your entire organization so that employees understand and accept their roles as part of an organization-wide security ecosystem. When you create this type of corporate culture—and pair it with holistic Insider Risk monitoring systems that are efficient and effective—we believe you've got a much better chance of containing the greater Insider Risk problem and protecting your company's data.

CHAPTER 5

The Digital Transformation Imperative

The more digital transformation enables data access and collaboration, the more exposed the organization is to Insider Risk.
—Joe Payne, President and CEO, Code42

Digital transformation is occurring in every sector of the economy. Every business and every organization must innovate at speed to stay relevant to its audience. From manufacturing to service organizations, from software development to research institutions, digital transformation is now table stakes to compete and thrive. This chapter zooms in on several relatable examples, including the YMCA. As the YMCA of the Greater Twin Cities that serves the Minneapolis and St. Paul area of Minnesota expanded its mission, the technological and security framework that supported collaboration became even more critical. With fourteen locations, 220,000 members, and hundreds of programs across the 3.6 million people in the Minneapolis/St. Paul area, the YMCA must remain nimble in helping its members, many of whom are part of vulnerable populations.[71] [72]

YMCA managers and employees depend on access to data to do their jobs. Members trust "the Y" to ensure that their information is secure and that they can conveniently and easily access in-person and online programs. A YMCA might not seem like a candidate for digital transformation—it's not a big manufacturing, finance, or technology company. However, the YMCA of the Greater Twin Cities operates in the throes of digital transformation, as does virtually every American organization. It's either transform—or get left behind. Leaders and boards everywhere are realizing that digital transformation drives organizational goals in an effort to compress time to innovate, time to market, time to revenue, and—most important—time to elevate the customer experience.

These values are just as important to the YMCA of the Greater Twin Cities as they are to other organizations. Just as everyone had to pivot to digital solutions when Covid-19 lockdowns began, the YMCA of the Greater Twin Cities had to quickly move their programs online to meet members' needs. That transition meant that members needed digital access and that YMCA employees needed the ability to solve problems and do their jobs without the frustrating restrictions that some security software brings. In fact, the YMCA's ability to pivot quickly would mean that members could enjoy a wide variety of livestreaming programming.

Not only can YMCA members access live fitness training and fitness classes from home, they can also join virtual cooking, book, and knitting clubs. Instead of acting as a poor replacement for in-person activities, the transition to digital created new ways of reaching the community and filled a need that previously hadn't been served.

When the state and local jurisdictions began to allow limited reopening, collaboration technology and security were just as crucial. To comply with Covid-19 occupancy limitations and keep members posted as to those capacity limitations, the YMCA launched a location capacity status dashboard. Members could quickly check to see if their nearby location had any availability or if they needed to go a different branch.

As the YMCA of the Greater Twin Cities demonstrates, digital transformation is the connective tissue of today's modern organization. There's no doubt digital transformation removes many innovation barriers so that organizations of all sizes can serve their customers and get products and services to market more efficiently. That's the good news.

The bad news? Insider Risk. In Chapter 4, we established how the digital transformation inherent in the collaboration culture can leave organizations vulnerable to Insider Risk. Unfortunately, conventional security approaches aren't meeting this challenge.

This chapter showcases the digital transformation imperative, the ways in which digital transformation leads to Insider Risk, and how digital transformation has created a disconnect between the c-suite and the CISO. For digital transformation to truly succeed, the CISO has got to be on board—which means giving the CISO a seat at the transformation table.

> **Digital transformation inherent in the collaboration culture can leave organizations vulnerable to Insider Risk.**

The Digital Business Imperative

Growing evidence suggests that digital transformation *and* a collaboration culture are necessary to secure a competitive advantage. That's exactly what countless organizations throughout the country strive to achieve. They need the ability to align digital transformation with their collaborative culture to achieve their business objectives. That means removing barriers to data to drive success. That's why the vast majority of CEOs in 2018—82 percent— prioritized digital initiatives and budget, a significant increase over the 62 percent who did so in 2016.[73]

PwC asked CEOs to grade themselves on the company's use of data to drive digital business initiatives.[74] They compared how CEOs responded based on two factors: comprehensiveness and criticality. In other words, how do the quality and quantity of the data collected and analyzed translate to actual digital business success? In answering this question, the CEOs surveyed identified the five biggest data gaps:[75]

- Customer needs
- Brand recognition
- Industry peer comparable
- Risk exposure
- Employee needs

Examination of these gaps reveal a correlation between digital transformation and the growing Insider Risk problem. After analyzing the 2019 and 2020 CEO investments in comparison to these gaps, it's clear that a majority of spending is going to close critical gaps in digital data capabilities, drive workforce productivity and efficiency, and place data at the center of the organizational culture. Each of these areas received at least two-thirds of newly allocated budgets.

When spending budget to move the needle around specific problems such as digital capabilities and organizational speed, your workers and your culture must embrace that change. Otherwise it won't take.

That's why talent and culture are such important components of digital transformation. And it's why 80 percent of enterprises will change their culture by 2021 as a way to accelerate their digital business strategy.[76] It's also why 89 percent of CEOs feel that their culture directly impacts the bottom-line metrics of their organization.[77]

> **Eighty-nine percent of CEOs feel that their culture directly impacts the bottom-line metrics of their organization.**

The YMCA of the Greater Twin Cities shows that the potential for digital transformation isn't confined to large technology companies. Let's look, for example, at this dynamic in a company in the health-care-services industry. BAYADA Home Health Care is a trusted leader since 1975 in providing clinical care and support services at home for children and adults.

BAYADA developed an innovative, proprietary electronic training simulation curriculum for its clinicians, who needed secure access to training on the go. Whether they are at home, in the office, or working in a client's home, their clinicians need to access these simulations to continually stay in touch with the latest home healthcare innovations. The company's clinicians also need methods to securely access and update patient records from the patients' homes to ensure appropriate care and continuity of care. The same patient may receive care from multiple clinicians, so it's critical that each clinician is up to date on the patient and any changes that have occurred in their condition, prescriptions, or treatment. An openness to digital transformation meant that BAYADA was able to leverage technology to keep up with the needs of patients and clinicians while staying competitive within the home healthcare industry.

The technology also facilitated easy access to data and training for BAYADA employees, enabling them to get their work done. For BAYADA, collaboration technology is instrumental in the fight to keep its most valuable assets: its team of trained workers and its proprietary data.

So, Who Owns the Organization's Culture?

Ultimately, the CEO defines the culture in digital transformation. That culture has three distinct but related components: people, technology, and data. While the CEO defines the culture, they turn to the chief human resources officer (CHRO) to develop the talent, and the CIO to enable the technology and data sharing. This isn't surprising, considering people and technology are two of the top three digital business enablers. Corporate Executive Board's Future of Work 2019 study found that when it comes to driving employee engagement, development, and growth, technology is the number one lever to pull—more than skills, rewards, or recognitions.[78]

> **While the CEO defines the culture, they turn to the CHRO to develop the talent, and the CIO to enable the technology and data sharing.**

In fact, 73 percent of CHROs believe that significantly changing the technologies employees use for work will drive engagement and enable growth.[79] This not only aligns with the CEO's digital business enablers and investment priorities, it also meshes with the CIO's top priorities. That's why 70 percent of CIOs plan to invest in an employee collaboration platform by 2023.[80]

Technology is where CIOs and CHROs find common ground, which is why so many CEOs anoint them as digital transformation change agents tasked with shaping the collaboration culture. Why? Because, collaboration culture drives results. According to Deloitte's Global Human Capital Trends 2019, nearly one-third of organizations have adopted a collaborative culture and more than half—53 percent—of those organizations have seen significant results. Results associated with bottom-line metrics like time to innovate, recruiting and retaining talent, customer experience, growth targets, revenue, and profits. But, it's not always rosy. The more quickly organizations move and the more freely employees collaborate the more vulnerable they are to risks—risks that manifest inside the organization.

Digital Transformation and Insider Risk

To clearly identify the relationship between digital transformation and Insider Risk, we asked security leaders in our Code42 2019 Data Exposure Report what variable was contributing the most to increased data security threats. Their answer? Culture. As we mentioned in Chapter 2, of the CISOs surveyed, 89 percent believe the fast-paced culture model of their organizations puts them at greater risk of data breach.[81]

Half of CISOs identified employee actions as the leading cause of data breaches.

Not only that, but 77 percent of CISOs report that the most significant risk to organizations is workers ignoring data use policies to do their jobs.[82] Half of CISOs identified employee actions as the leading cause of data breaches, while 45 percent identified third-party insiders—contractors, partners, and vendors—as the culprits.[83] Contrast that with the 28 percent who cited external actors such as cyber criminals and malware as the main sources of a data breach.[84]

We had to validate what CISOs say is actually what employees admit, and you know what—CISOs are spot-on. The more digital transformation enables data access and collaboration, the more exposed the organization is to Insider Risk. What we found is that Insider Risk is most heightened when employees decide to leave the organization:[85]

- 63 percent of employees admit to taking company data to a new job
- 70 percent of employees took data less than thirty days before they resigned
- 66 percent of employees admit they took data to help them get their next job

Yes, the statistics are overwhelmingly high. Let's look at an example to bring those surprising numbers into focus. You may not think about digital transformation as a necessity for competitive advantage within the Heating, Ventilation, and Air Conditioning (HVAC) industry. But the case of MacDonald-Miller, an HVAC contractor in the Pacific Northwest, will prove you wrong. The team at MacDonald-Miller leveraged collaboration technology to develop a game-changing MLAB, a 750-square-foot virtual reality cave that allows customers to experience their projects before they are actually built. MacDonald-Miller design engineers and architects collaborate with customers in the MLAB to share the art of the possible, optimize designs, make adjustments in real time, and fast-track the project to rollout and completion.

What makes the virtual reality cave so innovative is that customers can actually see what their projects will look like and how they will change the buildings that they are placed within. Unlike two-dimensional architectural and construction blueprints, virtual reality is a powerful tool that speeds the design process, reduces the potential for costly errors, and facilitates faster collaboration and decision making.

MacDonald-Miller created its unique virtual reality simulator to attract new customers. If MacDonald-Miller's proprietary technology fell into the hands of a competitor, this technology would no longer be unique and the company would lose a critical competitive advantage. This is not just some theoretical musing—this is exactly what almost happened. An employee from MacDonald-Miller's IT department was hired by a competitor. On the way out the door, he copied sensitive data critical to the MLAB. Had MacDonald-Miller not had the right security technology and processes in place to spot the illicit activity, they would have lost their competitive advantage. They successfully balanced the sharing and collaboration culture needed to create sustainable advantage with the security tools and processes

to track when/if someone abused the trust placed in them. "Trust, but verify" served MacDonald-Miller well—and, of course, made security a hero
with the CEO, but this is not always the case.

Insider Risk Disconnect

YMCA of the Greater Twin Cities, BAYADA, and MacDonald-Miller are
exceptions to the norm. The truth of the matter is most CISOs simply do not
see Insider Risk through the same lens as the digital transformation examples we shared. According to our "Voice of the CISO" research, CISOs' top
three security strategy and budget priorities are regulatory compliance, protection of structured data, and malware. End-user—employee—risk and
workforce culture changes make up the bottom of their list. No wonder
Insider Risks are on the rise.

The disconnect between our research and information security priorities led us to sit down with a group of CISOs to gather context and try to
understand their reasoning. What we found is that most of them define the
insider threat narrowly. How? Specifically, they told us that "insider threat
is the use of social engineering by an external actor in order to compromise
an internal user and gain access to the corporate network and thus data."[86]
No mention of employees, contractors, and freelancers as actors who compromise data based on their own actions. When we requested clarification,
they typically offered two different rationales:[87]

1. "Insider threats posed by employees is not a big enough
   problem to solve."
2. "What we have in place is good enough for employee-driven
   insider threat."

CISOs agree that insider threats pose risks to their businesses, but
believe that their current strategies are sufficient to deal with the data risk.
In other words, CISOs view their current level of Insider Risk as acceptable.
Also, they have strong faith that their current technology stack composed of
broader monitoring and data loss prevention (DLP) will protect them from
risk. Ultimately, their stance is that dedicated Insider Risk technology
designed for employee theft and misuse of data are redundant. In other

words, it isn't necessary to create strategies and allocate budget toward mitigating Insider Risk because first of all, it isn't much of a problem, and second of all, they've already got it covered.

Wait a second! These beliefs directly contradict our quantitative research, which identified the collaborative culture, employee entitlement, and employee responsibility for Insider Risk as some of the organization's top priorities. Here's the disconnect—while CISOs identify digital transformation as a cause of heightened insider threat, they fail to prioritize Insider Risk solutions in their strategies and budgets.

> **While CISOs identify digital transformation as a cause of heightened insider threat, they fail to prioritize Insider Risk solutions in their strategies and budgets.**

Digging deeper, we reviewed the research with them and discovered the root of the problem—external forces. So, it's not exclusively the CISOs' own personal sentiment toward Insider Risk; they are subject to external forces that push them in that direction. CISOs identified three areas that drive their security strategy and budget prioritization and thus, the Insider Risk disconnect:[88]

1. External security requirements, including regulatory, customer privacy, insurance underwriting
2. External security assessments that identified gaps in specific areas
3. External consultations with industry analysts, peers, resellers, and service providers

This means that CISOs—at an essential level—rely on third-party mandate and consult to shape their strategies and budgets. Let's face it, external attacks and ever-evolving regulatory compliance are top of mind for most CISOs because the threat is tangible and visible. They see the alerts. They know what external attacks they've blocked. It's hard to blame CISOs for their position because when it comes to Insider Risks, the threats are largely invisible, going undetected for months or even years. As digital transformation and collaborative cultures become ubiquitous across organizations, this lack of detection—lack of visibility to Insider Risk—drives CISOs to look inward to better balance collaboration and risk. We traced the growth of the collaboration culture and the growing Insider Risk problem to three core employee realities:

- **Data entitlement**: 72 percent of employees believe their work files are their property[89]
- **Data exploitation**: 63 percent of employees admit to taking data from a past employer to a new job[90]
- **Data portability**: Eight of the top ten data exfiltration vectors are cloud-based[91]

Given the attitudes of employees around data—entitlement, exploitation, and portability—and the growing Insider Risk challenge, shouldn't the CISO and information security in general be at the center of the digital culture transformation? Shouldn't the CISO offer a proactive security strategy to future-proof the collaboration culture?

Productivity and Security Go Hand in Hand

Just talk to the YMCA of the Greater Twin Cities. In order to strengthen the community, which is the organization's cause, the YMCA believes it's important to make it easy for employees and volunteers to do their work in supporting its programs and services—and data security plays a vital role.

For the YMCA of the Greater Twin Cities, the importance of data security lies in its ability to keep data safe while enabling its users to get their jobs done efficiently and fast. If its users aren't able to access their data, it impedes their ability to accomplish the organization's mission. Specifically, data loss means time wasted redoing work; it means time spent researching where data went; and it means determining whether that data movement created risk for the organization.

The YMCA of the Greater Twin Cities realized that security and collaboration must work hand in hand for the organization to succeed. The organization also knows that if data security presents too many roadblocks, its employees will stop using organizationally sanctioned technology and use their own personal apps. To meet the need for collaboration and security, the YMCA embraced a more proactive Insider Risk solution that offered continuous monitoring and rapid detection and response.

Then there's Shape Technologies Group, the leading innovator in water-jet cutting solutions based in Kent, Washington. With a growth target of $1 billion, SHAPE is moving quickly to achieve that goal through strong organic growth and a global acquisition strategy. When SHAPE buys a company, the sell-side company's IP is a core part of the value proposition. Unfortunately, that data is easily put at risk by employee actions and departures. That's why it's critical for SHAPE to secure that IP as they onboard and integrate new employees and assets.

Achieving economies of scale by consolidating operations is a key part of SHAPE's M&A strategy. As the company takes steps to achieve these efficiencies, layoffs may be needed. Because of this, SHAPE is diligent about safeguarding both owned and acquired confidential and proprietary data from Insider Risk. The company has a lot of IP, and it needs to make sure it's not walking out the door.

For BAYADA Home Care, protecting its proprietary training programs while remaining HIPAA compliant were critical security concerns. Because BAYADA's workforce is highly dispersed, providing care services in clients' homes, the organization needed to ensure a secure environment regardless of where their employees were working. One of the company's main challenges was lack of visibility into the laptops that traveled outside its network. BAYADA is a very decentralized company, and seeing where the data was stored was a challenge. Anticipating the potential for Insider Risk, BAYADA put the right tools and technology in place to manage and mitigate potential threats.

These progressive companies demonstrate that securing the collaborative culture is not only possible, it's also essential. Without appropriate security precautions, BAYADA would risk heavy HIPAA fines and potential exfiltration of its proprietary training program. Just like BAYADA, the YMCA of the Greater Twin Cities concluded that a traditional security solution would not work. By focusing on securing their collaboration culture, the YMCA enabled its employees and community to continue to access high-quality fitness programs before and during the pandemic. In the same way, Shape Technologies Group can fearlessly pursue its M&A strategy with the knowledge that proprietary data at their acquisition targets will be quickly secured should a deal go through. Three unique organizations with three unique digital transformation initiatives, all embracing that collaboration and security go hand in hand.

Conclusion: Add the CISO to the Culture Table

Clearly, it's past time for the c-suite—specifically the CEO and CIO—to partner with the CISO to not only make their digital transformation initiatives successful, but also secure. It's time for the CISO to claim their seat at the corporate-culture table.

When it comes to the collaboration culture, if the CEO defines it, then:

- The CIO (technology) enables it
- The CISO (security) protects it
- The GC (legal) oversees it
- The CHRO (people) shapes it

Moving into chapters 6 through 8, you'll learn how specific roles such as the CIO, CISO, legal, and human resources can cooperate effectively to secure the collaboration culture. In Chapter 6, we showcase the CIO and the CISO, who play a central role in not only facilitating digital transformation, but ultimately securing it. In Chapter 7, we feature the general counsel, who offers strategic advice and legal perspectives designed to support both collaboration and security. Chapter 8 celebrates the CHRO, who builds an effective employee experience to both shape and secure the corporate culture.

Let's turn to Part 2: The Change Agents of the Collaboration Culture.

PART TWO

The Change Agents of the Collaboration Culture

CHAPTER 6

The Progressive
Information Officer

To turn [a] progressive vision for security into reality, the CIO and
CISO both need a seat at the decision-making table.
—Jadee Hanson, CIO and CISO, Code42

To create successful digital transformation and a collaborative culture, two
executives are key: the CIO and CISO. That doesn't mean that the c-suite
and organizational workers aren't critical to achieving business objectives—
they are. However, the CIO and CISO are pivotal figures, the organizational Velcro who both enable and secure the collaboration culture.

As we've shared in the first half of this book, digital business transformation requires a fast-moving, collaborative culture. At the same time, the
speed of that culture puts organizational IP at risk.

Even when insider breaches don't take down an organization, they can
provide an unnecessary distraction. As you'll learn in Chapter 7, investigating and litigating Insider Risk cases is expensive and time consuming
and may not achieve a satisfactory result. Empowering both your CIO

and CISO is one of the best ways to avoid a rear-view mirror approach to Insider Risk.

We've seen what happens when Insider Risk runs amok in organizations. Remember SunPower? The company experienced three major insider breaches during the past decade. Because SunPower lacked the mindset and tools to appropriately address Insider Risk, incidents kept occurring. These weren't small issues, either. As a result of these repeated exfiltrations, SunPower sued former employees and competitors, including SolarCity, SunEdison, and Standard Industries, in 2012, 2015, and 2019.[92] [93] [94]

The most recent lawsuit charges that a former executive vice president of global channels "forwarded emails containing proprietary sales information to a personal account and drafted a PowerPoint presentation called 'Solar Overview for Standard' based on SunPower's proprietary and confidential information," according to Reuters.[95] Ouch.

While we don't know exactly what the data loss prevention platform looked like at SunPower, we've seen enough ineffective programs at other organizations to have a good idea of what goes on. Usually, as we discussed in Chapter 4, the situation involves an overreliance on blocking and classification systems that aren't very good at containing insider threats. Almost always, this information security culture is a throwback to the past—not only in the information security functions themselves, but also in the c-suite. Yesterday's insider threat information security environment clearly needed a significant upgrade. That job falls upon the CIO and CISO. To effectively secure the collaborative culture, the CIO and CISO must step into the leadership void and accept their role as powerful change agents.

> **To effectively secure the collaborative culture, the CIO and CISO must step into the leadership void and accept their role as powerful change agents.**

What does empowering CIO and CISO change agents look like? Several common threads run through a progressive approach to IT and security, as we'll explore in more depth later in this chapter:

- Assume positive intent
- Ensure organizational transparency
- Establish acceptable data-use policies
- Deploy Insider Risk technology
- Provide training and awareness across the organization

To turn this progressive vision for security into reality, the CIO and CISO both need a seat at the decision-making table. Though CIOs tend to be the visionaries implementing collaboration technology, unfortunately, many CISOs are sidelined from executive decision making because they are seen as a roadblock—instead of a facilitator—of digital transformation innovation and collaboration. That will change when CISOs show that they understand the imperative of digital transformation and c-suite leaders realize that security must permeate organizations for that transformation to succeed.

In this chapter, you'll learn about the transformation of the CIO and CISO roles that facilitate digital transformation, the collaborative culture, and truly modern Insider Risk platforms. Under the leadership of the CIO and the CISO, progressive security teams must work within their organizations to minimize Insider Risk and maximize data security awareness. Security and IT teams are best positioned for success when their leader, in many cases the CISO, has a seat at the executive decision-making table. Getting there requires a shift in mindset on behalf of the CISO and executive leadership. All partners on the executive decision-making team must buy into the concept that the collaboration culture and data security are two sides of the same coin.

Yesterday's Insider Threat Culture

Consider this scenario. Following a massive data breach that exposed the personal information of millions of members, an insurer fell victim to insider threat. The incident involved an employee who allegedly misused member data. In investigating the incident, the insurer found that this employee emailed a file containing members' personal information—including names, dates of enrollment, Social Security numbers, and health plan ID numbers—to a personal email address. If you're still not sure what

Five ways organizations find out that they were breached by an insider:

- **Customers**
- **Competitors**
- **The media**
- **Law enforcement and legal**
- **Risk assessment or audit**

insider threat looks like, this incident is a textbook example. In many cases, incidents like this can take months to identify. During that time, the personal information of thousands of people is at high risk.

Many insider breaches take months to come to light. This is a common experience. Verizon found that 73 percent of data breaches go undetected for months if not years.[96] This type of incident occurs all too often due to outdated insider threat platforms that rely on blocking and classifying to manage Insider Risk. Most of these systems simply do not work effectively, so most breach management happens long after the breach occurred.

Yesterday's Information Leaders

Managing information security in today's collaboration culture can be a thankless task. At the same time that CISOs are trying to protect their organizations, CEOs, CIOs, and their c-suite partners are adding potentially problematic—from the security perspective—platforms and tools to speed the corporate culture.

In the past, the CISO and the CIO frequently found themselves at odds. While the CIO supports the CEO's collaborative-culture vision by adding tech designed to facilitate collaboration, the CISO focuses on mitigating risks involved in that collaborative tech. The CIO, who, by the way, is often the CISO's boss, views the CISO as stubborn and uncooperative. That results in sidelining the CISO from decision making, leaving the CISO in the position of securing tech that they don't like, trust, or believe in.

This dynamic tends to spiral in many organizations, leading the c-suite to view the CISO as a business blocker. The CISO, frustrated, then tends to double down on their views, further widening the gap between information and security. This situation ultimately results in relegating the CISO to an organizational subbasement, where they futilely attempt to battle Insider

Risk with inadequate blocking and classification tools. The c-suite, meanwhile, charges ahead in their digital transformation efforts. The average tenure of a CISO is less than eighteen to twenty-four months, and it is no wonder why.[97]

Unfortunately, when the entire c-suite is at odds with the CISO, it's the organization that suffers the most. Sure, jobs will get done. Deliverables will be met. Employees are productive. However, that disconnect can't help but surface. Maybe those organizations will get away without an insider threat incident. But it's not likely, and it's not in the best interests of the organization in the long run. The most likely outcome is one—or more—insider threat incidents like those at Jawbone and SunPower.

Progressive CIOs

The best CIOs effectively bridge the gap between the architects of the collaboration culture and the architect of the security culture, the CISO. These CIOs understand that collaboration and security must be mutually supportive for the goals of the organization to succeed. Without collaboration, achieving a competitive advantage is impossible. Without security, maintaining that collaborative culture and competitive advantage is also impossible.

To achieve the goal of securing the collaborative culture, CIOs partner with CISOs on organizational business objectives, facilitating the CISO's understanding of *why* these objectives are important and *how* they will position the organization for success. The progressive CIO treats the CISO as a partner in enabling the organization to thrive.

When the organization needs new tech to support a collaboration goal, such as improving the employee experience, the CIO involves the CISO in selecting the platform that will achieve HR's goals in a secure manner. Through these experiences, the CISO matures in their understanding of the organization goals, and learns how to effectively support these goals while keeping the company and its data safe.

Empowered by the CEO, the CIO is tasked with the responsibility of providing technology to facilitate organizational collaboration, including customer relationship management, HR, finance and legal apps, as well as those that span the organization, including the Google Suite or Microsoft

Office 365. Cloud-based sharing apps such as Box, Dropbox, Microsoft OneDrive, and Google Drive are also essential. As the owner of organizational technology, the CIO is a crucial change agent in ensuring that the CISO is brought along to do their part in effectively securing the collaboration culture.

Collaboration Culture Change Agents

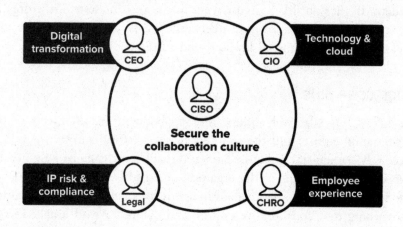

Progressive CISOs

The evolution from traditional to progressive CISO occurs over time as individual CISOs learn—by trial and error—how to take responsibility for securing the collaborative culture.

Progressive CISOs are made, not born. The evolution from traditional to progressive CISO occurs over time as individual CISOs learn—by trial and error—how to take responsibility for securing the collaborative culture. All the aspects of a healthy Insider Risk program that we've discussed so far are part of the progressive CISO's mission—assuming positive intent, providing transparency, and establishing customer-first Insider Risk policies.

Truly progressive CISOs go beyond the traditional role of identifying risks and taking a hands-off attitude toward problem solving. When CISOs see themselves as part of the solution, they move to a proactive posture by designing Insider Risk programs that manage risk while helping executives, managers, and workers accomplish their collective and individual business goals. That happens through creating partnerships and building empathy, to gain an understanding

> **The Progressive CISO's mission:**
>
> • **Assume positive intent**
> • **Provide transparency**
> • **Put customers first**

of how others deliver work and the struggles they contend with in trying to get their jobs done.

For example, Code42's security team learned coding. The team did that as part of its collaboration with company developers to help identify and address security gaps. When our security team members learned some coding language, they gained a fuller understanding of the challenges developers face every day. They also learned how they need to work with developers to be part of the solution.

Longtime CISOs understand that it's impossible to eliminate risks. The job is more about *balancing* risks. Think about a Walmart. There's the risk that everything out on the store floor could be stolen. But you can't lock everything down, or the company won't make any sales. Because Walmart and other retailers are in the business of selling goods, they can't lock up everything. Instead, they take other precautions to minimize theft.

The same calculus is true of all business risks. You must balance the business benefit with the business risk, while putting reasonable risk mitigation practices into effect. For example, a retailer such as Walmart might choose to minimize the risk of theft with security cameras, security guards, and locking away items that have a high risk of theft. This is something else experienced CISOs understand—we can't place overly aggressive security controls on everything, including data and proprietary information. Our job is to fine tune to the right level of security, given an organization's business and culture. That involves balancing what the board, CEO, line-of-business leaders, and customers want and need. Security leaders who are overfocused on their own agenda tend to make the mistake of pushing forward with their own rigid security posture ideals versus trying to genuinely understand the acceptable-risk posture of an individual organization. Hence the reason CISOs need a seat with the c-suite.

The best CISOs understand that they are only as strong as their security team. Relying on experienced, empathetic security personnel allows the CISO to confidently implement a progressive Insider Risk program, because they know they can rely on the team to execute their vision. This type of team can more easily earn the trust of their non-security coworkers, leading to organizational buy-in on security objectives. A well-tuned, committed, and effective team translates to a more effective Insider Risk program. Not only that—but it makes it much easier to retain talent in an industry where good talent isn't easy to find. When a CISO has a trusted team, security is much more effective and laser focused on the overall mission of the organization.

The most effective, progressive CISOs share four important qualities:

1. **Possess a clear vision**: For your vision to come to life, you need everyone in the company to get on board with it and keep it top of mind on a day-to-day basis. That means articulating your message in a repeatable, relatable, and doable message. In brief, that means repeating your security message in different ways at different times and aligning your vision with your organization's corporate culture.

2. **Listen, listen, listen**: To effectively lead, you must know who you're leading and what's important to them. In today's remote work environment, that means joining every Slack or Microsoft Team channel available so you're tuned in to what's on employees' minds.

3. **Demonstrate appreciation**: Frequently thanking employees for specific achievements through email and all-channel communication fuels the fire for everyone to continue to work together to keep the company secure. In an office environment, tangible gifts such as gift cards, donuts, and pizza are always appreciated.

4. **Empower teams**: Trust that you've hired the best security team. Communicate and train them so they can operate at their highest capacity.

Take a Seat at the Table

It's clear that to gain a seat at the table, CISOs must be seen as proactive business enablers, rather than rules-obsessed business obstructors. Obtaining and maintaining a seat with the c-suite means that CISOs must both deliver technical solutions designed to protect their organization and make a positive contribution to solving complex business problems.

In order for an Insider Risk program to succeed in the long run, CISOs must have the support of business leadership. That's because it's up to an organization's leadership to provide an Insider Risk program with the continuous funding it needs as well as the political backing to overcome any speed bumps that arise.

Unfortunately, many CEOs, CIOs, and line-of-business leaders tend to sideline CISOs because of a perception that they aren't on board with the need for speed in digital transformation and collaborative culture initiatives.

However, even before unveiling the most effective tools and processes to manage Insider Risk, CISOs must demonstrate a firm grasp on organizational digital business objectives. CISOs must understand those goals and get behind them. Unfortunately, many CEOs, CIOs, and line-of-business leaders tend to sideline CISOs because of a perception that they aren't on board with the need for speed in digital transformation and collaborative culture initiatives. Whether that is true or not in any given organization, CISOs need to pass a loyalty test to gain support. That means showing up and getting involved in as many key business strategies as possible.

And yes, this takes time and energy. Schedules will fill up and there will be many Zoom meetings unrelated to the CISO's key functions. However, they actually are directly related, because in order to secure the digital business culture, the CISO must live and breathe that culture and those priorities. Any CISOs who hide out in their metaphorical security subbasement, glued to their security monitors, will remain on the outside of the c-suite.

However, CISOs who commit to radically and consistently increasing their visibility will appear on the c-suite's radar. Then the CIO and the rest of the c-suite be willing to listen.

To obtain and maintain that support, CISOs must explain the real-world risks in a way that executives can understand. Put together a presentation that uses real-world case studies and data designed to zero in on the problem in plain English. Shining a light on Insider Risk and how it impacts business risk with the executive team can help CISOs articulate their value to the company. Working through exercises that determine how easily specific risks can be exploited, and sharing that with key decision makers, goes a long way toward helping executive leadership understand the *why* behind your budget requests. It's also critical to level with executive leadership about security risks, instead of overhyping them to get attention or budget. This short-term tactic can definitely backfire by diminishing trust in the long term.

To gain ongoing funding and support for an Insider Risk program, it's important to build a persuasive case so that executive leadership can easily understand the risks and the most effective solutions. Remember, securing and maintaining funding are two different issues. It can be easier to secure funding for a shiny new object—especially when that object is technology—than it might be to continue funding in the face of new, competing budget objectives. The best way to continue to solidify support and ensure that funding is maintained is to keep Insider Risk fresh in the eyes of the executive audience. This can include:

- Regular, brief updates on big-picture Insider Risk trends, news, and research
- Regular, brief reports highlighting the success of your Insider Risk program, including:
  o Highlighting positive (and negative) data—again, be transparent
  o Emphasizing money, time, and energy saved versus money, time, and energy spent

Of course, support beyond the c-suite is also important. Other critical stakeholders include legal and HR. When building effective data security and Insider Risk management processes into your employee life cycle, close collaboration with legal and HR must occur. More on this in chapters 7 and 8.

Build a Sustainable Security Culture

No Insider Risk program or software solution will prevent all data from risk of exfiltration. It is the CISO's and security team's job to educate the c-suite and employees on security risks and foster an appropriate security culture. In other words, how do workers act in regard to data security?

> **It is the CISO's and security team's job to educate the c-suite and employees on security risks and foster an appropriate security culture.**

What does building a strong security culture involve? In a healthy security culture, employees take personal accountability for keeping data safe. Everyone thinks twice before clicking on links. They proactively message, email, or phone security if they have security questions. When they're interested in using a new product or service to get their work done, they will reach out to security about the risks. In practice, a solid security culture looks something like this:

Jeff: *There's a new plug-in that we could install in this app to improve the UX.*

Stacey: *Great! Where is it from?*

Jeff: *Heard about it on the CodeBuddies Slack channel.*

Stacey: *What does security think?*

Jeff: *I Slacked them and they are checking it out.*

> **A strong security culture acts as a pillar for an effective Insider Risk program.**

A strong security culture acts as a pillar for an effective Insider Risk program. Imagine if employees would "say something if they saw something," to borrow a line from Homeland Security. Most staff, if they see a peer sharing a document out of policy or in an unsecure way won't say anything at all. Why? Because they aren't trained how to say something to help coworkers do the right thing. An effective security culture removes barriers to acting appropriately.

When building an Insider Risk program from scratch, start small, keep it simple, and remain open to making changes. Early wins are important and will help drive the success of the program. Chapter 9 includes many frameworks and templates you can adapt to build a stronger Insider Risk program.

Fundamentally, building a sustainable program that evolves over time is about continually managing data exfiltration and Insider Risk. This task may seem straightforward—and it is—but that doesn't mean it happens easily or quickly. As we mentioned up front in this chapter, effective insider threat programs should include the following elements:

- Assume positive intent
- Provide transparency
- Establish acceptable data-use policies
- Deploy Insider Risk technology
- Increase awareness
- Offer training

We'll go through these step-by-step.

Assume Positive Intent

The most effective method for driving digital transformation while building a collaboration culture is through assuming positive intent. What does that mean? That means operating with a positive mindset when dealing with Insider Risk alerts and issues. Instead of coming down on your employees like Big Brother, you can pick up the phone and ask questions. Here's an example:

Bob in security: *Hi Amy, this is Bob from security. We noticed that you downloaded some company contracts onto a thumb drive. Just wanted to see what was going on.*

Amy the paralegal: *Really? I didn't mean to do that. I had accidentally downloaded some family pictures from our Disney cruise onto my company laptop and wanted to get those off. Since they were big files, I used a thumb drive. I must have clicked on those contracts by mistake. What should I do? I'm really sorry!*

Bob: *Disney cruise? That sounds like fun! No worries, Amy. If you could delete those documents from your thumb drive and send me a screen shot of the contents of the thumb drive showing that they aren't there anymore, we can close out this incident. Thanks so much for your cooperation.*

Amy: *Of course! I'll do that as soon as we get off the phone. I don't want to cause any problems.*

When an organization as a whole and security in particular assume positive intent, employees are much more likely to cooperate and trust their intentions. Instead of approaching Amy with suspicion, Bob came at the security issue with a positive mindset and was able to bring it to a conclusion without alienating a valuable employee or escalating an issue that was fairly simple.

Provide Transparency

Transparency begins with making sure all employees understand during their onboarding that the organization monitors all data movement. Part of this process involves explaining *why* such monitoring is important—and that is because the organization's data, proprietary intellectual property, and business viability must be protected. If data is leaked intentionally or unintentionally, the future of the company is at risk, which could mean the loss of a competitive edge and revenue.

In Chapter 3, we noted that as far as Insider Risk is concerned, there is no difference between good, bad, or indifferent intent. Risk is risk, no matter what flavor it comes in. Insider Risk isn't about bad employees—Insider

Risk happens when the well-being of the organization is at stake, regardless of the intent. By emphasizing transparency and trust, instead of punishment, security teams can relate to their employees as allies rather than adversaries.

Organizations can take this one step farther by inviting employees to join in the effort to protect organizational IP. That means fully educating them on the dangers of Insider Risk and their specific role in protecting data.

Establish Acceptable Data-Use Policies

An integral part of a credible Insider Risk program is establishing acceptable data-use policies. When workers know what's permitted, what isn't permitted, and why, they can relax and get their work done. The more specific your policies are, the better. Examples help, too! Here's one:

> *All of Company XYZ's documents, data, and information that you access on a company device in the office or remotely is automatically backed up to our Amazon Cloud account. That means that you won't lose data that you work on. Our Amazon Cloud storage account is the only authorized cloud backup service available. Do not back up your company data or work to unauthorized cloud storage systems such as Box, Dropbox, or iCloud.*

As you create these policies, make sure that they answer common questions that employees ask, including:

- Can data be moved to USB devices and other local, removable storage devices?
- Can data be shared on corporate collaborative platforms such as Slack or Microsoft Teams?
- What's the policy for taking data home?
- What's the policy for keeping data on a company or personal laptop, tablet, or smart phone?
- What's the policy for sharing company data with outside contractors/vendors?
- Who owns the intellectual property that I've created while working at the company?

Executives, managers, employees, contractors, and freelancers need clear rules around what are acceptable uses of the organization's systems and data and who owns the organization's information. Employees must be reminded of these policies on a regular basis. More on that shortly.

Deploy Insider Risk Technology

While much of your Insider Risk program will consist of data security policies and employee awareness and training, technology is a necessary component of a successful program. Without technology, there is no way to monitor the effectiveness of your policies. Technology that focuses on monitoring file movement, rather than employee actions, is most effective at mitigating Insider Risk.

> **Technology that focuses on monitoring file movement, rather than employee actions, is most effective at mitigating Insider Risk.**

When considering the types of tools that will support your Insider Risk program, choose the solution that provides the capability to detect, investigate, and respond to data breach incidents with the appropriate level of insight. Any credible Insider Risk technology should have the ability to assess:

- User-based risk: Full visibility for rapid Insider Risk detection and response
- Organizational-based risk: Continuous data collection and protection to mitigate risk during mergers and acquisitions, litigation, or other organizational restructuring events
- Device-based risk: Instant file recovery that protects from lost or stolen devices, ransomware, and other disasters
- Cyber risk: Comprehensive visibility that enables proactive threat-hunting of external cyber threats lurking within the organization

Insider Risk solutions should operate with a simple, automated workflow. That begins with the capacity to collect and monitor files and file activity for all users and every device. Then, they should help security teams quickly and easily identify suspicious behavior and rapidly investigate.

Finally, they should enable security to access the exact file or files in question, determine risk, and respond within seconds. These capabilities should possess file breadth, depth, and access designed to deliver smart outcomes with efficiency, efficacy, and speed.

Integration also is a huge part of a successful Insider Risk technology deployment. The most successful integrations function smoothly within your existing internal processes and existing tool sets. For example, if you have an established automated employee off-boarding process, can you connect this process to your Insider Risk program so that you have timely, accurate insights into employee status changes? The same holds true for employee onboarding.

As we have disclosed previously, our expertise comes from working for a data security company, Code42. We've built cloud-based software from the ground up to these specifications. We are so confident you will appreciate the approach we have taken to Insider Risk that we invite you to try it for yourself at no cost. Find more at www.code42.com.

Increase Awareness

Awareness consists of education about Insider Risk in general and specific insider threats likely to arise within your organization. Helping your executives, managers, employees, contractors, and freelancers understand the importance of the risks you're trying to manage will help them understand the rationale behind your Insider Risk program.

> **The best types of awareness programs seek to partner with employees to create a shared sense of responsibility for organizational security.**

The best types of awareness programs seek to partner with employees to create a shared sense of responsibility for organizational security. In other words, a feeling that everyone is in this together. When every individual within your organization takes responsibility for their part in managing Insider Risk, you're much less likely to encounter insider threat incidents. As we've previously mentioned, communicating to workers that the company's proprietary information is what keeps it in business helps reinforce this sense of joint responsibility.

Emphasizing that everything that everyone creates while working at an organization belongs to that organization sets expectations around entitlement and ownership. When organizations make it repeatedly clear that all intellectual property belongs to the company—not the individual or team who created it—there are no blurred lines. That doesn't extinguish Insider Risk, but it helps manage expectations.

Offer Training

Appropriate and ongoing security training is critical to the success of any Insider Risk program. Ongoing training programs build "muscle memory" for all workers across the organization. Any training program should reflect organizational corporate culture.

While there are many packaged Insider Risk security training programs, those may or may not be suitable. At Code42, we looked at a few of these packaged solutions. One included videos that were thirty minutes long—like anyone would watch a thirty-minute security video!

Many of the other packaged training videos we reviewed fell short of getting important messages across to our employees, focusing too much on unlikely, sensationalized scenarios. Even if you have an insider threat problem, how likely is it that it involves your sales manager handing bulky envelopes of privileged information to shady strangers outside a nearby restaurant? Not very!

Instead of buying a packaged solution, we made our own security video. It was easy. It was designed to get the basic information across to employees, while treating them as professional collaborators in securing our corporate culture. To that end, we sought to get four important points across that we wanted employees to internalize and act on:

- **Get ahead of risks**: If you have a business reason to move data outside Code42's environment, please let us know beforehand.
- **Protect our data**: Data that's created at Code42 belongs to Code42 and should stay within the helpful Code42 collaboration software provided to you to help you do your job.

- **Don't use personal storage**: Did you know that adding personal storage accounts to your work device could accidentally result in Code42 data being uploaded to your personal account? It can and it has happened before.
- **Ask before you take**: Personal photos are yours, and you should have those. If you're planning on departing, just inform the security team and your manager as to what you wish to take with you before you move it. That way we'll all be on the same page.

For example, in a six-minute-and-thirty-two-second video, we provided background on Insider Risk, let our workers know what their responsibilities are, and clarified what they could and couldn't do. Obviously, there's way more to say about this topic, but it doesn't take too long to get the major points across. This is just one way that we at Code42 eat our own cooking. Obviously, as a data security company, it's essential that everyone who works here understand security best practices. (By the way, we give this video away to any organization that wants it for no cost. Just ask us for it.)

Because of our dual mission as a data security company—to secure our customers' data and our own information from Insider Risk—we created a Security Ninja program, which teaches security principles while requiring positive security behaviors on the job. See Chapter 9 for a complete framework of the program that you can use in your organization.

Implement Proactive Policies Today

Insider Risk is not going away—in fact, it's only getting worse. If you have an insider threat program and haven't taken steps to modernize it with the elements we outlined in this chapter, *now* is the time. If you are just getting started with a new Insider Risk platform, this is the perfect opportunity to design the launch of that program with these progressive elements in mind.

In the first half of this book, we shared some incidents with you such as SunPower and Jawbone that showed what happens when organizations lack visibility into Insider Risk. In Chapter 7, you'll learn more about the lengthy legal life cycle involved in investigating Insider Risk once data has been exfiltrated. Fortunately, by adopting the right technology and taking all the appropriate steps to support that technology, it will be easier to cut the time it takes to investigate and remedy Insider Risk incidents.

Two of the most important stakeholders in any Insider Risk program are legal and HR. In the next two chapters, we offer hands-on advice for general counsels and CHROs about how they can productively contribute to establishing a security culture.

Insider Risk Program Checklist:

- **Assume positive intent**
- **Provide transparency**
- **Establish acceptable data-use policies**
- **Deploy Insider Risk technology**
- **Increase awareness**
- **Offer training**

CHAPTER 7

The Progressive General Counsel

As corporate culture has evolved to accommodate speed and collaboration, legal must adopt the same proactive stance demonstrated by the CISO, CIO, CHRO, CEO, and line-of-business leaders.
—**David Huberman, General Counsel, Code42**

To sustain competitive advantage, organizations must continually innovate while securing intellectual property against Insider Risk. The general counsel—and the entire legal team—are critical components in protecting your organization in today's collaborative culture.

Formerly, legal and the general counsel were relegated to a technical compliance function. The c-suite—and the rest of an organization—viewed legal as a sleepy corporate backwater. Like security and HR, legal was rules-based and negatively oriented. Playing it safe, the general counsel and the legal team were extremely risk averse. Legal was another "land of no."

Today, legal has transformed into a critical partner in facilitating digital transformation and managing Insider Risk. As corporate culture has evolved to accommodate speed and collaboration, legal must adopt the same proactive stance demonstrated by the CISO, CIO, CHRO, CEO, and line-of-business leaders. That requires flexibility, creativity, and cooperation with the rest of the c-suite. Seen from this perspective, the general counsel is a true collaborative-culture change agent.

Collaboration Culture Change Agents

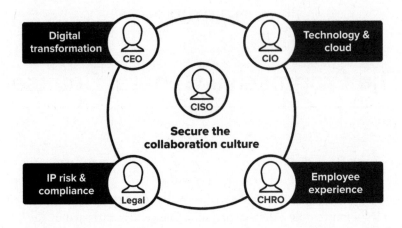

Legal's role in safeguarding your organization is both outward and inward facing. Legal is not only responsible for staying up-to-date with constantly changing local, state, national, and international regulatory and legal environments, but also for ensuring the organization remains compliant. The legal team must sift through a vast array of constantly changing rules and standards to determine how to best safeguard your organization while also helping it navigate the environment and thrive.

In this chapter, we'll cover how—and why—legal has transformed into an essential strategic partner within the c-suite from a formerly defensive-oriented posture. We'll also go over the ways that legal can help protect your organization against Insider Risk and how that contributes to digital transformation.

Yesterday's Legal Environment

Traditionally, the legal department's role in mitigating Insider Risk began and ended with non-compete and nondisclosure agreements. In many organizations, these legal documents are still viewed as an indispensable get-out-of-jail-free card. Bring up the subject of Insider Risk with many general counsels and we guarantee you'll hear some iteration of: "We have every employee sign a non-compete and a confidentiality agreement when they are hired, so legally, we have Insider Risk covered."

These legal arrangements are ubiquitous in intellectual-property-rich industries like tech, pharma, consulting, manufacturing, and government contracting firms. They are also popular among research institutions such as higher education. If you're perched up in a legal ivory tower, non-competes and confidentiality agreements seem like the answer to all of your Insider Risk problems.

In yesterday's traditional work environment, these documents were likely enough to put a lid on Insider Risk. In the absence of the Internet and collaborative technology, it was much more difficult to remove a company's proprietary data. However, in today's collaborative culture, such documentation is no longer enough. The work environment is too open and dispersed for the risk of future legal action to work as a deterrent.

Before we get to all the effective techniques for managing Insider Risk from the perspective of the general counsel and the legal team, we'll explain more about what non-competes and nondisclosure agreements are as well as what they can and can't do. While organizations probably won't stop using them and requiring employees to sign them, it's simply a mistake to rely on them exclusively to protect you from Insider Risk.

The function of non-compete and nondisclosure agreements is to create legal obligations for workers and demonstrate their knowledge of those obligations. While employees, contractors, and freelancers do sign them— they've got to, if they want to start their jobs—their significance frequently gets lost amid the piles of paperwork that they typically execute as part of the HR onboarding process. With their eyes glazed over from either actually or virtually signing reams of paper, many pay scant attention to the significance of non-competes and nondisclosure agreements.

The true value of these documents is realized in court, should an insider threat situation get so far out of hand that you end up there. At that time, the documents—signed and dated by the worker who allegedly committed the insider breach—will be introduced as key evidence in the case. So what's the problem? As you'll see in this chapter, the courts don't really like non-competes. Also, by the time you get an insider threat case to court, it may be too late. More on that later.

Back to basics—in essence, a non-compete agreement is a contract between an organization and its workers that restricts the ability of workers to join competing firms. As a tool to mitigate Insider Risk, these agreements are designed to achieve the following results:[98]

- Protect trade secrets
- Reduce worker turnover
- Increase costs for competitors
- Create leverage with workers

Confidentiality or nondisclosure agreements are also contracts between organizations and their employees, freelancers, and contractors designed to protect organizational intellectual property from disclosure to competitors.[99] Confidentiality agreements specify what information is confidential and not, as well as the consequences of disclosing confidential information. Such agreements are designed to accomplish the following goals:

- Detail each party's responsibilities
- Retain a competitive advantage
- Create standards for handling data
- Protect intellectual property

Unfortunately, the protections of both non-compete and nondisclosure agreements are largely illusory. Why? Judges aren't fond of non-competes and interpret them very narrowly. Enforcing non-competes in the courts is difficult, expensive, and time consuming. Not to mention they are limited or presumptively invalid in several jurisdictions. States like Illinois, Maine, Maryland, Massachusetts, New Hampshire, Oregon, Rhode Island, and Washington have made non-compete agreements unenforceable.[100] Others, like Florida, Utah, and Connecticut, have put into place enforceability restrictions by profession. For example, non-competes are unenforceable when it comes to salaries below $100,000 or within certain professions, such as healthcare.[101] States that permit non-compete clauses typically stipulate that the restrictions in the agreements must not exceed the employer's legitimate business interests.

Not only are courts increasingly unfavorably disposed toward non-compete clauses, the federal government is also taking steps to rein them in. The US Department of Justice and the Federal Trade Commission have increased scrutiny of non-compete agreements.[102] In 2016, the Department of Justice warned organizations that it planned to carefully examine and potentially criminally prosecute non-poach and wage-fixing agreements between employers. An FTC public workshop in January 2020 explored the issue of whether the agency should issue a rule designed to restrict the ability of organizations to impose non-compete agreements.[103] Also on the federal level, a bipartisan coalition of federal lawmakers has proposed a bill entitled the Workforce Mobility Act that would eliminate non-compete clauses in employee agreements. The only potential exceptions include partnerships and business sales.[104]

Both state and federal moves to restrict or eliminate non-compete clauses reinforce the premise that you can't rely on these instruments to protect you when it comes to Insider Risk. On the other hand, while confidentiality obligations are generally enforceable, they're still difficult and costly to enforce, and when you do enforce them, you're doing so after the fact. Many organizations have a misconception that non-compete and confidentiality agreements are a strong deterrent of Insider Risk. As a practical matter, they provide a very limited defense.

Many organizations have a misconception that non-compete and confidentiality agreements are a strong deterrent of Insider Risk. As a practical matter, they provide a very limited defense.

In certain types of cases, nondisclosure agreements become controversial. During the #MeToo controversy of 2018 and 2019, many female employees who charged that their employers sexually harassed them lost the ability to disclose this harassment due to nondisclosure agreements in connection with financial settlements. For example, Michael Bloomberg, CEO of Bloomberg and former US presidential candidate, was attacked for his company's extensive use of nondisclosure agreements when settling claims of sexual harassment and workplace discrimination.[105]

As a result of these controversies, some organizations have ended their use of nondisclosure agreements within the context of settling discrimination and harassment claims.[106] A number of states, including New York, Maryland, Tennessee, Washington, and Vermont, restrict nondisclosure agreements in employee contracts. New York's law, which was passed in 2018, requires that settlements in sexual harassment cases can't include a confidentiality agreement unless the victim wants one.[107]

These controversies reveal how vulnerable both non-competes and nondisclosure agreements are. Not only are they under attack by many states, but they can cause reputational damage. And did we mention that they don't do much to actually prevent Insider Risk? Fortunately, there are more proactive strategies that will actually protect your organization against Insider Risk, which is up next in our explanation of how to construct a legal security culture.

Building a Legal Security Culture

Now that you know what not to do, it's time to delve into what you can do to secure the collaborative culture. There are a number of approaches you can take to counter Insider Risk through compliance, context, and transparency.

Compliance

When it comes to Insider Risk, the minimum legal must do is simple: comply. Comply with any legal and regulatory requirements in the relevant jurisdiction. Compliance is what it is—a checkbox. It's not, however, a strategy. It's not a catalyst for collaboration, innovation, and growth. And it's not the answer to managing or mitigating Insider Risk. It's a variable to take into consideration as you build your Insider Risk strategy, program, processes, and technology stack. Remember, compliance won't keep your trade secrets safe.

> **Compliance is what it is—a checkbox. It's not, however, a strategy, and it's not the answer to managing or mitigating Insider Risk.**

That said, there are important regulatory considerations to take into account when combating a growing Insider Risk problem. These considerations center on three key variables: information, location, and employee. Each of these variables play a role in answering critical questions, such as:

- What data is needed?
- Where does it exist?
- How do we use it?
- Who has access to it?
- Why is it needed?
- When is it no longer needed?

In the United States, generally speaking, employees have no expectation of privacy when using corporate assets. In the absence of any comprehensive federal action on data privacy, however, the states are acting by creating a patchwork of data privacy statutes that may diverge from the long-standing position that employees using company equipment don't enjoy privacy rights. Perhaps the most well-known state privacy law to date is the California Consumer Privacy Act (CCPA), which "grants California consumers data privacy rights and greater control over their personal information, including the right to know, the right to delete, and the right to opt out of the sale of personal information that businesses collect, as well as additional protections for minors."[108]

The CCPA does not currently extend each of these rights to employees. The law focuses on the protection of the consumer, and organizations in possession of consumer information must comply. Several other states have proposed similar legislation. Some statutes, such as those proposed in Washington and New Hampshire, would cover all personal information held by an organization, including information collected in the employee-employer relationship. Again, make sure to be aware of the laws of states in which you operate as regulations evolve in definition and scope.

Elsewhere, regulations like the General Data Protection Regulation (GDPR), which covers countries within the twenty-seven-member European Union, govern what personal information employers can use and retain. At a high level, GDPR established a number of principles around the need for consent and usage.[109] With it, rules for data retention help answer the question, "When is it no longer needed?" with affirmative obligations to either anonymize or purge data.[110]

Given the evolving privacy landscape, legal must have a solid handle on where all corporate data resides and the justifications for retaining it for a specific period of time. In order to meet these requirements, you should conduct periodic data-mapping exercises so you can answer the question, "Where does data live?"

Context

We've spoken with a number of outside counsel to get their perspective on the trials and tribulations of Insider Risk. What we learned is that the foremost legal pain stems from the fact that Insider Risk is almost always a game of turn back the clock. Organizations struggle to answer what happened—what data was taken—three, six, nine, or even more than twelve months ago. Therein lies the frustration and the pain. It's all too likely that your organization won't know data was compromised by an insider until you see it in the news, hear it from law enforcement, lose a big deal or contract, or catch wind of a competitor launching a product or service that looks oddly similar to one on your own road map. Because it's a constant game of turn back the clock, when an insider breach is discovered, the process that confronts the legal team is long, labor intensive, and expensive.

> **What we learned is that the foremost legal pain stems from the fact that Insider Risk is almost always a game of turn back the clock.**

To start the process, legal—in partnership with IT—must obtain the computer the insider used. Once the computer is obtained, it is turned over to a third-party forensic analyst to gather evidence around the event. A forensic analysis on a single device can cost many thousands of dollars and take weeks to complete, and time is a luxury organizations and their legal teams don't have when it comes to investigating intellectual property breaches. The more time that goes by, the more expensive and laborious the investigation gets, and the more damage there is to the business and brand. Even if the forensic evidence makes your case and you win the lawsuit—years later—it's a Pyrrhic victory because you've already lost business or, worst case, you've gone out of business. We saw this with Jawbone. Fitbit may have been their competition, but time was their enemy.

Practically speaking, we prefer a game plan that takes a more proactive approach. When it comes to investigation and response to Insider Risk—whether it be the legal team, security, HR, or line-of-business managers—context is everything. As a legal team, in the event an employee—an insider—has taken, leaked, destroyed, or outright misused company data, you want to know:

- Who did it?
- What data did they take, leak, destroy, or misuse?
- When did it happen?
- How did it happen?
- Where did the data go?
- If it was a former employee—where did they go?
- Why did they do it?

All of this context matters because it dictates how your organization responds and what actions you need to take. Security's job, for instance, is to understand the what, when, how, and where of the incident. Your security team must be able to detect when everyday work poses credible risk to the business and the brand.

Your legal team, on the other hand, will be focused on the employee and the intent—the who and the why. As we discussed in Chapter 3, the security team should not care as much about the who and the why. Financial and reputational damage falls into the legal team's realm and the context behind who was involved and why becomes critical.

The reason is because "the who and the why" will dictate the response. In Chapter 3, we discussed the various profiles of the insider—good, bad, and indifferent. Each insider has an underlying context that dictates the response, whether it be driven by legal, HR, or the employee's manager.

Remember Tom the Saver? He's the extremely organized and risk-averse product marketer who saves everything. Because Tom saves everything, he syncs all of his work files on his company-issued MacBook to iCloud. It doesn't bother him that iCloud isn't a company-sanctioned app. He figures that as long as he delivers quality work on deadline, the company should be satisfied. However, because he pulls down work files at home on his own iMac and iPad Pro, the company's supersecret product road map is now sitting out there on his iCloud account. That's risky. From security's viewpoint, the employee is putting data at risk—big risk—and legal needs to understand who and why.

The "why" context behind Tom's activity tells legal, HR, and his boss that Tom needs more coaching. The response is not to reprimand Tom, block him from doing legitimate work, or fire him. The response is sending him an email or a Slack message, calling a quick meeting, or assigning him additional security-awareness training. If Tom continues to ignore policy and put corporate data at risk, thus more context, then the response may need to be more serious. Most employees mean well. Truth be told, there are times when technology and policy get in the way of getting work done. Being proactive means IT and security teams appreciate and accept the way people work. It also means IT and security teams can provide the much-needed context to legal should everyday work become an Insider Risk to the business or the brand.

Transparency

Transparency goes both ways. We will give you a personal anecdote. To celebrate a family milestone, one of our employees wanted to put together an eight-minute iMovie photo montage of his son from birth to the present day. Photos, music, transitions—a whole production—so we're talking a big file needing a lot of storage and processing horsepower. So, being transparent, the employee reached out to IT because his work laptop was the fastest computer he had. "Hey, can I download iMovie onto my Mac to work on this personal project?" IT said yes. He worked his iMovie magic and got to the point where he needed to share it with somebody via Google Drive. Knowing that the device was being monitored, he emailed the security team. "Hey, just a heads-up, I'm about to upload a large file to my personal Google Drive. This is what it is and why I am doing it." Security appreciated the heads-up. Had he not been so transparent, security would have undoubtedly raised the red flag to the manager, legal, and HR. A giant file with a bunch of individual files zipped together then uploaded to a personal Google Drive account—on a Saturday—equals a huge red flag. Sound the alarms. No doubt, security double-checked to make sure it was not corporate data, but still appreciated the transparency. Transparency is a best practice when it comes to Insider Risk.

Transparency is a best practice when it comes to Insider Risk.

The Progressive General Counsel

Now that you understand how to approach Insider Risk from a best-practices approach, how do you execute these strategies? By being a progressive, strategic, and collaborative general counsel conversant with Insider Risk. Like other members of the c-suite, the general counsel must move the needle strategically from the "land of no" and reliance on non-compete and nondisclosure agreements to a legal and security culture based on transparency. That means proactively collaborating with the CIO, CISO, and CHRO to identify the best technology to execute an Insider Risk program while backing up that tech with clear and complete policies, procedures, training, and communication.

As we've shown you, Insider Risk is a complex, multifaceted problem. That's why Insider Risk containment programs must be flexible, clear, and complete. It's no accident, then, that a highly skilled, strategic executive is required to participate in building such a program. Executive recruiter Korn Ferry lists the skill sets of an efficient and effective general counsel:[111]

- Integrating legal strategy throughout an organization
- Enabling business outcomes

- Assuming strategic business responsibilities
- Building strong internal and external relationships
- Resolving complex business challenges
- Focusing on value-added tasks
- Delegating and mentoring legal talent

Examining all these facets of the general counsel's role is beyond the scope of this book. However, there's no doubt that these attributes are essential when managing Insider Risk and collaborating with the c-suite in containing Insider Risk.

The General Counsel and the C-suite

Employees at Code42 see this disclaimer every time we log into our corporate-issued computer:

> *This system is monitored, recorded and audited for carefully considered, specific and targeted purposes. Your use is consent to these legitimate and proportional activities. Unauthorized use may be subject to criminal and civil penalties.*

Any employees needing more information on exactly what tools we're using and what we're monitoring can consult our employee privacy statement. When it comes to Insider Risk, privacy and security go hand in hand.

This disclaimer is a prime example of c-suite and cross-functional team collaboration. To create this disclaimer and the privacy policies that back it up, security, IT, legal, and HR teams worked together to facilitate as much transparency as possible from the cultural and privacy perspectives. Why? Because your entire workforce should understand the laws that your company is subject to and why they are important.

Protecting the business and the brand from Insider Risk also takes transparency and collaboration. It's not exclusively a security problem. Security, IT, legal, HR, and every line-of-business leader have a stake in the game. Transparency is critical for building a culture that values security. Employees should know—from day one—that your organization tracks file activity. They should understand that the program is applied universally without privileges or exceptions—and they should understand how the program is designed to support their productivity while protecting the business.

Because privacy is evolving, as a legal team, you will need to work with security, IT, and HR to understand what data your organization's technology is collecting. If you are considering employee-monitoring software like User Activity Monitoring (UAM) or User Behavior Analytics (UBA), legal needs to be part of setting buying requirements from a compliance perspective. In a similar fashion, HR needs to be involved setting buying requirements from a culture and employee experience perspective. More on that in Chapter 8.

As your organization rolls out new and upgraded technologies and policies, continue to maintain that transparency across departments and the employee base. Make sure you document all the ways you collect information about employees and your purposes for collecting the information. Notify employees about the information you are collecting and why you're collecting it. We've found transparency pays a major dividend: it's a big deterrent of Insider Risk in and of itself.

Finally, every time new Insider Risk technology, processes, programs, or policies are being considered, legal must have a seat at the table and a voice in the decision. Establish a regular routine with stakeholders to audit existing technology, processes, programs, and policies, and keep them up to date. Given the fluidity of the regulatory landscape, Code42 established a semiannual review. Every six months, legal sits down with security, IT, HR, and line-of-business leaders to review our Insider Risk program, the processes, and the technology. The outcomes of these bi-annual meetings dictate updates to our privacy statements and any related employee documentation, customer documentation, product documentation, and partner or vendor documentation. Doing so ensures we strengthen our Insider Risk posture, while also checking the appropriate boxes to remain compliant with ever-changing regulations.

Cross-functional insider threat data questions

Securing the collaborative culture with transparency requires a cross-functional effort. To get started, legal teams must work with key stakeholders across executive, security, IT, and human resources teams to get answers to these critical questions:

- Do you have visibility into all employees' off-network file activity?
- Do you know what data employees are moving, when they move it, and where?
- When someone leaves your company, what do you do to ensure they aren't taking confidential information with them?
- If one of your employees accidentally shared a file outside your organization, how would you investigate to determine whether you had any reporting obligations to regulators or customers?
- Do you know what trusted and untrusted collaboration tools employees are using?

Tomorrow's Evolving Legal Environment

Today's organizations are moving faster than ever. Propelled by the need to gain and maintain competitive advantage and fueled by external challenges such as Covid-19, there's no standing still. Amid the many challenges your organization faces, Insider Risk is one that can, at the worst, bring you down, or in the best case, divert necessary resources and damage your reputation.

That's why it's so important to use every talent and tool at your disposal to control Insider Risk while maintaining a collaborative culture that can continue to engage in digital transformation. You've learned about how the CEO, board, line-of-business managers, CISO, CIO, and general counsel contribute to this effort. In the next chapter, we will discuss the role of HR in ensuring the culture they've built does not fall victim to Insider Risk.

CHAPTER 8

The Progressive Chief
Human Resources Officer

> CHROs are most effective when they build and maintain
> an employee experience that aligns with core values,
> fulfills the need for digital transformation, and secures
> the collaboration culture against Insider Risk.
> **—Joe Payne, President and CEO, Code42**

As organizations grow more dynamic and knowledge-focused, the traditional command-and-control culture has quickly evaporated to be replaced by environments that offer more flexibility, creativity, and innovation. Employees are demanding more than a paycheck and standard benefits. They want work-life balance, flexible benefits, a sense of connection with their peers, and the tools necessary to collaborate. Consider someone like Amber, a millennial UX engineer ready to give her best on work deliverables, as long as she feels respected and that her organization shares her values.

To persuade Amber and employees like her to buy in and commit to their current organization, many companies must transform themselves. Impressive titles, competitive pay, and benefits are no longer enough.

Instead, values—and how those values are lived out by employees—matter most. The process starts with the CEO defining organizational core values. "Exceptional organizations have core beliefs that are unique, simple, leader-led, repetitive, and embedded in the culture," according to a Deloitte survey on core beliefs and culture.[112] The CHRO then takes those core values and uses them as a foundation for building a dynamic corporate culture and an employee experience that is fulfilling and relevant.

In this chapter, we explore how HR and the role of the CHRO have evolved and how progressive CHROs engage with their peers in the c-suite. CHROs are most effective when they build and maintain an employee experience that aligns with core values, fulfills the need for digital transformation, and secures the collaboration culture against Insider Risk. An effective collaboration culture serves as a guidepost for employee behavior. When there's no gap between what an organization says and what it does, employees know what to do and what not to do. We'll capture that journey and how you can recreate it in your organization.

Traditional HR

In a similar fashion to the traditional security culture that we discussed in Chapter 6 and the traditional legal culture we covered in Chapter 7, HR teams of the past were a process-and-control function that systemized recruiting, hiring, onboarding, and off-boarding. In managing an organization's human capital, HR ensured that as much value as possible was extracted from human capital by balancing compensation with performance and output.

HR focused on transactional and procedural functions, including facilitating onboarding and off-boarding paperwork and managing benefits, compensation, policies, and procedures. The HR team was primarily composed of administrators and clerks who shuffled papers, enforced rules, and made sure the paperwork train ran on time. HR was heavily rule focused.

While traditional HR functions must still be performed, those functions have taken a back seat to a more dynamic function: managing the employee life cycle and the employee experience. This shift has been supported by advancements in technology that have automated the tasks that HR used to have to manage manually. With the right technology, workflows can be created to ensure these tasks are completed, freeing up HR to proactively build and maintain a vigorous, values-oriented corporate culture.

Why Culture Matters

Clearly, the environment in which a progressive CHRO operates has shifted dramatically since the command-and-control days. Today's employees are selective about the companies they work for—for good reason. A Workfront survey revealed that 89 percent of employees surveyed believe their work matters, while 90 percent are proud of the work they do.[113]

Today's knowledge workers, just like Amber, seek to work at organizations that inspire them, that reflect and respect their values, and that allow them to make a difference. That's why they are selective about where they choose to work. Employees aren't satisfied with the status quo—they want an energetic, fast-paced, inclusive, diverse, and flexible culture. They're attracted to corporate cultures that prioritize collaboration and innovation so they can bring ideas to life and create products and services that make a difference.

That's not the situation, however, for nearly half of employees globally. Due to a variety of circumstances, more employees are disengaged than engaged. Gallup estimates the number of engaged workers rose to 35 percent in 2019, which indicates that 65 percent are disengaged or apathetic.[114] That lack of engagement spells trouble for maintaining a talent base, because highly engaged employees are 87 percent less likely to quit than their disengaged coworkers.[115] That's one reason why workers are changing jobs more frequently than ever, a trend that started shortly after the 2008–2009 recession and has continued to accelerate: Employee "quits"—voluntary departures—have risen every year since 2010, according to the US Bureau of Labor Statistics.[116] Another reason for the rise in departures is that a growing number of employees lack loyalty toward their employers. In fact, they switch jobs frequently in order to advance their careers and develop professionally. To retain the top talent that drives results in an organization requires a vibrant, responsive culture.

> **To retain the top talent that drives results in an organization requires a vibrant, responsive culture.**

When such a culture flourishes, workers, managers, and executives freely and easily collaborate, nimbly bringing fresh and exciting products and services to market that their customers value. These innovative products and services translate to improved bottom-line results. According to Mercer's 2020 Global Talent Trends Report, "companies that exceed their performance goals are three times more likely to have employee experience (EX) as a core part of their people strategy today, compared to firms not meeting their goals."[117] This isn't new—it's a connection that's been well established for nearly forty years. In "Bringing Corporate Culture to the Bottom Line," an article that appeared in *Organizational Dynamics* in 1984, research scientist Daniel Denison found that an effective corporate culture is associated with a significantly higher return on investment.[118]

Gallup research reveals that a highly engaged corporate culture is associated with a 10 percent increase in customer ratings, a 20 percent increase in sales, and 21 percent greater profitability.[119] Organizations with this type of culture share these common characteristics:[120]

- Defining core corporate values begins with the CEO
- Pursuing corporate culture as a competitive, strategic differentiator
- Communicating consistently and transparently
- Utilizing the right metrics to measure engagement
- Hiring and developing strong managers

This type of corporate culture pays another critical dividend, because it deters Insider Risk and fraud in general. Unfortunately, too many organizations pay lip service to corporate values. Executives and managers say one thing and do another. That's where fraud and Insider Risk gain traction. "We continue to see instances of fraud, corruption, and employee misconduct in corporate organizations where culture is an issue," said Holly Tucker, a partner with Deloitte Financial Advisory Services LLP in a *Wall Street Journal* Risk and Compliance Journal article.[121]

Mitigating Insider Risk, Deloitte noted, is a collaborative task best managed from a corporate-culture perspective. That means responsibility for both the corporate culture and Insider Risk is managed most successfully by cooperative teams from HR, legal, security, and IT. "There is cross-stakeholder ownership of both culture and fraud risk, and many executives should have a lens on both," observed Carey Oven, a partner with Deloitte & Touche LLP.[122] We'll explore what this looks like from the vantage point of the CHRO and the CHRO's collaboration with the CIO, the CISO, and the general counsel. Then we'll look at how it's specifically executed.

The Progressive CHRO

While there are many facets to the CHRO's role, in this section we focus on the aspects most closely related to Insider Risk. Unfortunately, even today, a vast majority of organizations don't have specific and consistent Insider Risk programs or processes to account for the unique data exposure risks surrounding the employee life cycle. In fact, we've found that only one in five organizations has a well-defined incident-response process for Insider Risk. With that in mind, we'll demonstrate how a progressive CHRO approaches three critical Insider Risk responsibilities:

> We've found that only one in five organizations has a well-defined incident-response process for Insider Risk.

- Creating data usage and security policies in collaboration with the CIO, CISO, and general counsel
- Building training around data usage and security policies
- Responding to Insider Risks inherent in the employee life cycle

Creating Data-Use and Security Policies

First and foremost, the CHRO must, in collaboration with security, legal, and IT, create a corporate data-use policy. There's no one-size-fits-all standard policy, because each organization deals with different types of data, intellectual property, and proprietary information. That's why an organization needs an explicit, written policy around employee data use, including:

- What they can and can't access
- Where they can and can't move data
- Who they can share the data with
- How they should go about getting permission to take personal files or data upon their departure

Your data-use policies—and other Insider Risk policies and procedures—must be clear and thorough. They must apply to employee activities throughout the employee life cycle, including recruiting, onboarding, development, retention, and exit or separation. They also must be comprehensive enough to deal with a variety of common Insider Risk scenarios such as:

- Sharing current work with colleagues through personal cloud accounts, collaboration accounts, and thumb drives to ensure projects keep moving forward and meet deadlines
- Transferring files to your home computer by sending them to your personal email account
- Saving and storing personal photographs on your work computer
- Deleting files to help "clean up" before exiting the company for a new job
- Moving customer and colleague contact lists to personal cloud accounts to use in future gigs

In Chapter 9, we'll share more tools designed to help your organization secure the employee life cycle.

When it comes to data-use policies, you can't relegate them to a dusty notebook in the back of an HR file cabinet. Instead, these policies must be alive, constantly adjusting to the reality of the current employee experience. That's where training and communication come in.

Building Training Around Data Usage and Security Policies

Training and communication start on day one for the new hires at Code42. As part of Code42's employee onboarding process, our new hires learn about the company's data-monitoring program. Informing employees about this program early on reinforces the message about transparency while serving as a powerful deterrent for data theft or misuse. Just as we don't want employees taking our data to other organizations, we also want to protect our organization from employees infiltrating data.

Many companies understand that, initially, new hires might bring data with them from other companies. So, we recommend walking new hires through your security policies and showing them how you monitor data and information to help them understand their role in keeping corporate data safe. We suggest mandatory trainings and policy sign-offs on an ongoing basis. You want employees to understand what your processes are, why security is important, and that your security approach is based on positive intent.

We recommend that you presume positive intent as a leadership team and a security team. Accidents happen and that is okay. As employees move beyond onboarding into the development and retention part of the employee life cycle—and move into new roles and have access to new information— you can help them understand the implications of their new access. Perhaps they now have access to data that is HIPAA or PII protected and they need training on compliance. Or maybe they are now managing people and have access to personal data about their employees.

In Chapter 6, we talked about the Security Ninja program at Code42. What started as a means for our security team to get employees up to speed on the security industry, technology, processes, and programs has evolved into a partnership between security and HR. We've taken our publicized data-use policies and processes and evangelized them through a rich employee experience that is fun and engaging. To date, nearly 80 percent of Code42 employees are Security Ninjas. You'll find more information about this program and how to implement it within your organization in Chapter 9.

Responding to Insider Risk Inherent in the Employee Life Cycle

It's up to the CHRO to ensure that Insider Risk triggers are established, practiced, and executed into workflows consistently. Establishing Insider Risk triggers should be a collaborative effort led by HR with support from the line-of-business leaders, security, legal, and IT.

> **Establishing Insider Risk triggers should be a collaborative effort led by HR with support from the line-of-business leaders, security, legal, and IT.**

How might this work in practice? One instance is embedding Insider Risk management within a new employee workflow. In most organizations, a new employee trigger or workflow automatically sets in motion an onboarding process that includes:

- Adding personal employee information to HR database
- Allocating resources, such as technology and office equipment
- Scheduling required training
- Setting up a new email address
- Creating salary and benefit accounts
- Providing access privileges

To cover specific Insider Risk, add specific security training and notifications about Insider Risk technologies to onboarding workflows. In addition, HR should work with security and legal to ensure new hires are not infiltrating data from a previous employer. HR should also define and establish a process around the departing employee trigger that automatically sets in motion an off-boarding process that includes a security analysis of the employee's data activity to look for potential exfiltration risks. Just like onboarding, this departing employee workflow should be followed for every departing employee.

Creating a corporate data-use policy checklist

It may seem obvious what data should be used for and who it belongs to—but it isn't, at least not to your employees. That's why you need to construct a corporate data-use policy and hold employees accountable to not only sign it but also understand it. Here are some issues to consider when building a data-use policy:

- What data is available
- What data is not available
- What data can be moved
- What data can't be moved
- Where to get permission to take personal data upon exit
- Who data belongs to
- Why data movement is restricted

Cross-stakeholder Collaboration

As Deloitte noted, cross-collaboration between the CHRO, CIO, CISO, and general counsel is essential to build and maintain a collaborative culture and secure that culture against Insider Risk. In this section, we'll look at how the CHRO collaborates with each of these partners.

The Collaboration Culture Change Agents

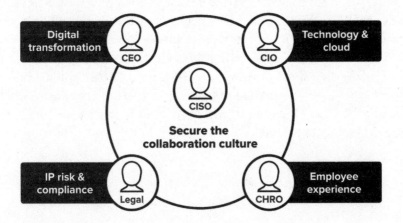

> **Cross-collaboration between the CHRO, CIO, CISO, and general counsel is essential to build and maintain a collaborative culture and secure that culture against Insider Risk.**

CIO

Technology not only enables business success, it also facilitates a strong corporate culture. But not just any technology—the right technology. In HR, that technology encompasses specific functions, such as:

- People management
- Policy and compliance management
- Shift scheduling
- Performance management
- Payroll
- Benefit management

As the guardian of corporate culture, however, the CHRO's interests in technology extend beyond HR-specific technology. The CHRO wants to ensure that all organizational technology aligns with corporate culture, a goal that can only be accomplished with the cooperation of the CIO. That means the CIO and CHRO must focus on business goals and processes and decide how to translate those goals appropriately for individual functions and teams.

Specifically, to ensure that HR technologies align with the CIO's vision, a dedicated IT Tech role could be embedded in HR so that IT can more fully understand what HR wants their technology to achieve. That IT Tech would also be tasked with educating about the capabilities of specific types of technology. In a similar manner, an HR team member could be embedded in IT to help IT understand the people aspects of non-HR tech. HR could also facilitate IT personnel strategies, identify talent gaps, and define future skill set requirements.

CISO

Because the employee experience and security depend upon each other, the CHRO and CISO are natural partners. Key intersections between these roles include:

- Securing the employee life cycle: HR keeps information security in the loop about emerging Insider Risk issues that occur in off-boarding and managing performance issues while information security helps HR design workflows to manage security aspects of the entire employee life cycle
- Protecting new HR technologies: Information security provides feedback on technology platforms and helps secure them
- Integrating HR technologies and security technologies to streamline processes and workflows
- Building training programs: Information security collaborates with HR on designing information security training

The CISO and the CHRO can collaborate through cross-functional teams. Since it's so critical to secure all aspects of the employee life cycle, an information security team member should be assigned to work with the HR team. In a similar fashion, an HR team member can be assigned to work directly with the information security team to mitigate the Insider Risk that can be inherent to people issues, such as hiring, training, performance, promotions, and benefits.

General Counsel

The CHRO collaborates with the general counsel to ensure that HR-related Insider Risk initiatives are compliant as well as that legal has visibility into Insider Risk.

HR and legal have many opportunities to collaborate. Here are some specific examples related to Insider Risk:

- Reviewing Insider Risk policies and procedures: Legal and HR can schedule regular reviews to ensure that Insider Risk procedures and policies comply with regulations.
- Establishing employee life cycle procedures: Legal and HR

can partner to identify the everyday employee life cycle events that trigger Insider Risks. Employee life cycle events include performance reviews, promotions and demotions, management changes, bonus payouts, and major organizational changes like a merger or acquisition, executive leadership change, organizational restructuring, and layoffs. See Chapter 9 on how to build an Insider Risk program around the employee life cycle.

- Providing transparency around data monitoring: Organizations that employ data monitoring to protect data from Insider Risk need to create transparent, legally compliant notifications so that employees are aware of the monitoring and how it impacts them. HR and legal can work together to ensure such notices are worded appropriately.

- If an insider breach actually occurs, the CHRO works with legal, IT, and information security to determine who is responsible for the breach, when it occurred, and the extent of the breach. Chapter 7 covered the painful and protracted process that results if there isn't continuous monitoring in place.

Building a Progressive Culture

The role of HR in today's collaborative culture involves identifying the best people, creating the best employee experience, and building the best culture. Creating an effective, functional, and enjoyable employee culture requires the cross-functional approach we just identified.

> The role of HR in today's collaborative culture involves identifying the best people, creating the best employee experience, and building the best culture.

Amber, the millennial UX engineer who you met earlier, just quit her job in disgust. Not only did she feel micromanaged, but her team also failed to deliver critical product upgrades on time. Why? A traditional security corporate culture rooted in blocking and policing left her little time to do her job. Instead, she spent part of her workday mired in endless arguments with security and IT about accessing data.

She's not worried about the rocky economy, because she knows her skills are in high demand. Instead, she's resolved to be highly selective about her next employer and determined not to waste her talents on an organization that isn't highly collaborative and transparent. Not only does she want to make a difference, she also wants easy access to the tools and apps that will make that possible. Amber also wants to make sure her future organization shares her commitment to integrity.

Amber is one reason why CEOs in search of business transformation rely on the CHRO and CIO to create the employee experience that will attract and retain employees like her. Even during periods of high unemployment, you need to hold on to your best employees and attract the best talent to fill your workforce gaps. That's why it's important to create a positive employee experience, which companies can do without compromising on Insider Risk. Here are three key elements of building a progressive culture:

1. **Employee training and development**: Engaged employees expect continual training and development. They want to succeed in their current roles and want to build skills and talents to continue to progress in their careers. To this end, progressive HR departments offer a variety of training and development opportunities to help employees successfully pursue the correct growth path. Leveraging technology to create such programs is a win-win because employees can consume training on their devices.

2. **Performance management**: Periodic performance reviews are all well and good, but to keep employees engaged, continuous performance management is more beneficial. In a continuous performance environment, workers continually share and receive feedback, monitor and achieve personal and team goals, and set and measure outcomes.[123] By replacing or at least supplementing a traditional annual-review approach with systems focused on development and agility, organizations

empower their workers to learn new skills. These new skills help employees move toward their goals and assist the organization in rapidly pivoting in new directions.[124]

3. **Work-life balance**: As we established in Chapter 2, today's employees prioritize achieving organizational objectives on their own terms. That's why they prioritize working with organizations that offer work-life balance. A progressive culture provides work-life balance through flexible schedules, a focus on productivity, workload reviews, volunteer opportunities, flexible benefits, support for caregivers, and time-off banks. HR should continuously review the menu of benefits and survey employees for their preferred options.

Nailing these aspects of creating a positive, nurturing corporate culture will help minimize Insider Risk. How? By turning employees into trusted, valuable allies, who are willing to go the extra mile to ensure that this culture is not victimized. As we've said before, everyone loses when Insider Risk makes the organization vulnerable. When employees understand this, they are less likely to breach this trust and more likely to remain valued partners.

> **Everyone loses when Insider Risk makes the organization vulnerable. When employees understand this, they are less likely to breach this trust and more likely to remain valued partners.**

Ride the Wave of Change

Organizations are in a constant state of change and that change almost always involves actions that impact employees—whether it's furloughing, moving positions from full time to contract, or a reduction in force. Mergers and acquisitions and crises such as Covid-19 are also changes that put employees on edge. And when they're on edge, they may make decisions with data that they might not otherwise make.

However, a positive, transparent corporate culture serves to mitigate this edge. It doesn't take the pain away from workforce reductions or a disruptive merger, but the trust built as part of a collaborative culture can help bridge the gap. That's especially true when insider threat security processes are consistent regardless of external change. When employees are aware that data is constantly monitored, they're less likely to take it. When employees are educated on best practices to keep data safe, there are fewer unintentional incidents. If a breach does occur, that monitoring will ensure that any malicious exfiltration will be more easily and quickly contained.

Up to this point, we've focused on the changes in corporate cultures that create insider threat and on the executive change agents tasked with facilitating a collaborative culture while managing insider threat. As we move into Chapter 9, we turn our focus to an overall Insider Risk security framework that you can use to protect your organization regardless of your size, market position, or industry. This workbook will guide you through many aspects of establishing an Insider Risk program designed around your organization's culture and objectives.

PART THREE

How to Secure the Collaboration Culture

CHAPTER 9

Insider Risk Frameworks for Securing the Collaboration Culture

> The promise of Insider Risk technology is to enable companies to detect and respond to data loss, leak, theft, and sabotage.
> —**Mark Wojtasiak, Vice President of Portfolio Strategy and Product Marketing, Code42**

For far too long, organizations have implicitly accepted Insider Risk as the price of the collaboration culture. The wild card in this scenario was the potential scope of the risk—best case, no data would leak; worst case, key employees would resign, taking highly valuable IP to a competitor. The more likely case? Some data would leak—hopefully data that wasn't too critical.

The most frightening aspect of this scenario is the unknown scope. An organization might never know exactly what or how much proprietary data was lost at what time. Or by the time they found out, the damage would be done. That's what happened to AMSC, global power technologies company, in 2011.[125] AMSC formed a partnership with Chinese wind turbine company Sinovel in 2010. Just a year later, in 2011, an automation engineering supervisor at AMSC secretly downloaded AMSC source code and turned it over to Sinovel, at the behest of Sinovel.[126] Sinovel then used this same source code in its wind turbines.[127]

The cost? AMSC lost more than $1 billion in shareholder equity and nearly seven hundred jobs, which accounted for more than half of its global workforce.[128] That's the bad news. The good news was that AMSC ultimately prevailed in court, as Sinovel was convicted of conspiracy to commit trade secret theft, theft of trade secrets, and wire fraud.[129] However, it took until 2018 for the case to conclude, seven years after the initial insider breach. Sinovel was fined $1.5 million, the maximum statutory fine over the theft. Sinovel settled an AMSC suit for $57.5 million.[130]

While AMSC won, it took seven long years and almost losing their business to emerge from an Insider Risk issue that could have been contained with appropriate detection and response technology. That's because Insider Risk detection and response technology is designed to quickly detect breaches, track down the perpetrator, and recover the missing data.

Unfortunately, even today, many organizations fail to adopt this simple solution. Instead, many are still operating in a prevention mode, relying on outdated blocking and classification systems to protect them from Insider Risk. These companies are still buying into a trade-off that they don't even need to make, risking key intellectual property in the service of a fully collaborative culture.

Today, this bargain is no longer necessary. Organizations can reap the benefits of a collaborative culture, which includes a rich employee experience, while containing Insider Risk. The promise of Insider Risk technology is to enable companies to detect and respond to data loss, leak, theft, and sabotage. In this chapter, we provide numerous nuts-and-bolts frameworks, checklists, and assessment tools designed to help organizations launch or refine their Insider Risk programs.

The frameworks we've included in this chapter are based on real-world journeys Code42 has experienced with our customers. They are designed to guide organizations in protecting themselves from Insider Risk, while complementing underlying Insider Risk technology. These frameworks are broken down into five core areas:

Section 1: Insider Risk Program Readiness Frameworks
Section 2: Insider Risk Program Assessment Frameworks
Section 3: Insider Risk Awareness Frameworks
Section 4: Insider Risk Response Frameworks
Section 5: Building an Insider Risk Team

Section 1: Insider Risk Program Readiness Frameworks
Questions CEOs, Business Leaders, and Boards Should Be Asking

In Chapter 2, we talked about how the evolution of people, technology, and data that has created the collaboration culture has also created vulnerabilities and Insider Risks not covered by traditional data security approaches. Given that, here are some questions CEOs, business leaders, and boards should be asking—and that CIOs and CISOs should be prepared to answer—about potential Insider Risk scenarios. Of course, this is not an exhaustive list. However, these questions will help create a baseline for assessing an organization's level of vulnerability and risk posture. How you answer the questions will serve as the foundation for your journey to securing your collaboration culture.

PEOPLE	TECHNOLOGY	DATA
When someone joins the organization, are you certain they are not bringing confidential information with them? How do you know?	Do you know what trusted and untrusted productivity, collaboration, and communication tools employees are using?	Do you have visibility to all file activity off the corporate network or VPN?
When someone leaves the organization, are you certain they are not taking confidential data with them? How do you know?	What technology and steps do you take to prevent misuse or misappropriation of your trade secrets by employees via personal cloud services?	Do you know at all times what files employees are creating, modifying, or deleting and how, when, and where it happens?
If you suspect an employee took confidential information to a competitor, how would you be certain? How long would it take? What would it cost? Would you have enough information to pursue litigation if needed?	If one of your employees accidentally shared a file outside your organization, how would you determine whether you had any reporting obligations to regulators or customers?	If an employee leaving the organization returned a wiped laptop, do you know for certain what information was accessed beforehand?
If an employee had his credentials compromised, could you detect if the account was being used to transmit confidential information outside the company?	What technology are you using to detect data misuse (either intentionally or accidentally)? How would you know if an employee took sensitive data? When would you know?	Which employees have access to your most sensitive information, including customer lists, source code, product road maps, and more?

Building an Insider Risk Program

In order to best manage and mitigate data loss, leaks, and threats, start by defining your own Insider Risk program, one that is rightsized for your organization. Here is our ten-step guide for CISOs and key stakeholders in legal and HR:

Step 1: Get Executive Buy-in

Don't fight this battle on your own. Getting definitive buy-in from leadership is the first and most critical step in establishing your security and IT team as value-added business partners—instead of data police.

Step 2: Identify and Engage Your Stakeholders

Continue the buy-in campaign from the top down. Think about which individuals or teams within your organization stand to lose the most from insider data theft or leakage. Identify and engage line-of-business leaders, HR, legal, and other IT leaders as key stakeholders in your Insider Risk program.

Step 3: Know What Data Is Most Valuable

Once you know who you're protecting, engage those line-of-business stakeholders in conversations about what data is most valuable to them. All data has value, but these conversations are essential to understanding the different types of unstructured data to keep a close eye on—and which types of high-value unstructured data will require more creative means of tracking.

Step 4: Think Like an Insider

With your valuable data in mind, put yourself in the shoes of an insider. Why would they want to move or take information, and what would they ultimately want to do with it? What tactics or blind spots might they exploit to do it? What work-arounds could they use to get work done? These are your indicators of compromise.

Step 5: Define Insider Triggers

Instead of building a monster program with classification schemes and policies that attempt to monitor every potential scenario—which are likely to ultimately fail—start by focusing on the few most common data exfiltration scenarios that impact nearly every organization: departing employees, high-risk workers, accidental leakage as well as organizational changes such as reorganization, M&A, divestiture, etc. These use cases make up the vast majority of insider threat incidents and serve as the foundational triggers of your Insider Risk program.

Step 6: Establish Consistent Workflows

Investigating suspected data exfiltration can be daunting. Once again, start small by focusing on the key use cases. For example, when an employee departure is triggered, define which activities will be examined—and which activities will trigger in-depth investigation. Exceptions and work-arounds are the Achilles' heel of Insider Risk programs. Make sure you clearly define the workflow for each trigger—and consistently execute and improve the steps you establish.

Step 7: Create Rules of Engagement

Once a workflow has been triggered and potential data exfiltration identified, it should be the key stakeholder's responsibility to directly engage the employee/actor. For example, departing-employee and accidental-leakage incidents will likely trigger engagement from HR and the line-of-business manager. An M&A workflow might trigger engagement from internal legal staff or the CFO. It's important that these rules of engagement segregate security and IT from any enforcement responsibilities. This allows them to focus on monitoring, detection, and remediation, and prevents security and IT from developing an adversarial "data police" relationship with staff.

Step 8: Leverage Existing Security and IT Teams and Train Your Stakeholders

It doesn't make sense for most small and medium-sized enterprises to create a fully dedicated insider threat team. Because we've honed the Insider Risk program down to a few key workflows, your existing security and IT teams should be able to handle the monitoring and detection responsibilities. But security and IT teams—who are already wearing multiple hats and managing strained resources—don't have to shoulder the full burden. It's also critical that other stakeholders—including HR, legal, and line-of-business managers—receive training so they understand the full scope of the Insider

Risk program: what is being monitored, the specific use case triggers, the investigation workflows, the rules of engagement, and the tools used to accomplish all of this. This training should also clearly define their roles and responsibilities, so they're ready to jump in when an incident-response workflow is triggered.

Step 9: Be Transparent in Communication

Transparency is critical for building a healthy culture that values security. Employees should know—from day one—that your organization tracks file activity. They should understand that the program is applied universally and without privileges or exceptions. And they should understand how the program is designed to support their productivity while protecting the business.

Step 10: Implement Real-Time Detection and Response Technology

Perhaps most important of all, your Insider Risk program must start long before a trigger. In other words, you can't afford to only monitor an employee's activity after he's given his notice, or after rumors of organization change have begun rippling through the office. Too many insider threat monitoring solutions are limited to this post-trigger scope—and far too often, the actual exfiltration occurs much earlier. True detection and response technology must be continuously running, providing historical context and complete visibility into all data activity. This enables your insider threat team to quickly and effectively see the full picture and protect your data.

A critical component of Insider Risk program readiness is understanding your blind spots. There is no better place to start identifying the everyday events that trigger Insider Risks to data than the employee life cycle. It's important to partner with HR to make sure you are taking the human element into consideration when developing each step of the program.

EMPLOYEE LIFE CYCLE				
ONBOARDING	COACHING & PERFORMANCE MANAGEMENT			OFF-BOARDING
Corporate policy agreements are not signed	Lower than expected merit increase or bonus	Unfavorable performance review	Low level of engagement	Voluntary departure
Mandatory trainings are not completed	Demotion	Performance improvement plan (PIP)	Internal or external job seeking	Involuntary departure
Files added to corporate device	Job transfer	Interpersonal conflict	Leave of absence	Reduction in force (RIF)
Device policy exception requests	Executive leadership change	Policy violations	Freelance or pro bono work	Layoffs
Unusual access requests	Direct manager change	Incomplete trainings or policy sign-offs	Mergers & acquisitions	Company reorganization

Section 2: Insider Risk Program Assessment Frameworks

Insider Risk Assessment Framework

Now that you've set a foundation for change, it's time to assess your readiness using our Insider Risk Assessment Framework. The Insider Risk Assessment Framework is designed for organizations starting an Insider Risk program from scratch and utilizing the technology investments they've already made. To complete your assessment, here is a recommendation for who should be involved:

- CISO
- Security Director
- Security Architect/Analyst
- HR
- Legal
- IT

What to Expect

Sixty to ninety minutes for discovery around your access, monitoring, and controls; employee life cycle management processes; and your security policies, governance, and agreements. Here is a list of questions to guide the conversation.

Access, Monitoring, and Controls

- Have potential Insider Risk incidents, scenarios, or triggers been identified?
- Have you defined what you are attempting to monitor and measure?
- Have you defined what information would need to be recorded or gathered in the event of an Insider Risk incident?
- Are your organization's solutions technically practical? Consider if the selected tools decreased "technical debt?"
- Have data-transfer protocols, such as FTP, SFTP, or SCP, been restricted to employees with a justifiable business need, and is their use carefully monitored?

- Has a response process been established when an event occurs? Who is involved?
- Is there a documented process or playbook available for the recovery of lost data or loss of access?
- What tools or processes provide visibility to the location and movement of your critical data assets?
- What tools or processes do you use to identify high-risk or departing employees exfiltrating data?
- Do you have a process or tools to determine if corporate policies for the handling of critical data are followed?
- Do you have a method to audit policy effectiveness?
- How do you currently look across your organization to track the movement of critical assets?
- What tools or processes do you have to recover user activity if you become concerned they may be misusing assets? How far back can you go to recover user activity data?
- Have you performed an audit recently? For what? Where were your biggest gaps? What are you doing to address these?

Employee Life Cycle Management

- Is your Insider Risk program inclusive of the following use cases: departing employees (exfiltrate), employee onboarding (ingest), high-value employees, unintentional data loss, nation-state actors?
- As part of employee separations (both voluntary and involuntary) are all nondisclosure and IP agreements reaffirmed?
- Are employees provided ongoing security-awareness training regarding Insider Risks specifically?
- For any user life cycle step (onboarding, departing employee) in your environment, do you have processes and controls to grant/remove access to appropriate assets/systems?
- Do you have a way to categorize and monitor data movement based on high-risk user groups?

- Is your Insider Risk strategy moving in the direction of alignment with external influences? (regulatory, industry, etc.)

Policies, Governance, and Agreements

- Does your organization have a defined Insider Risk Program?
- If so, how would you describe its maturity/capability?
- Have you defined your data critical assets or "crown jewels?" In selecting a response, consider if part of that process involved consulting with multiple stakeholders across the company.
- What level of executive support has been established?
- What level of stakeholder (e.g., HR, legal, business units) support has been established?
- Have specific policies and procedures around Insider Risk been defined (versus general InfoSec or IT)?
- Has your organization modified your security policies to identify proper data management and handling techniques for critical data assets?
- Has a data-transfer policy and procedure been created to allow sensitive company information to be removed from organizational systems in a controlled way?
- Has a removable-media policy been established and technologies implemented to enforce it?
- Has a cloud-usage policy been established and technologies implemented to monitor and enforce activity?
- Have processes for data backup been defined and communicated?
- Is ownership of data backup and recovery processes and associated playbooks defined?

Insider Risk Management (IRM) Maturity Framework for Collaborative Cultures

As we pointed out in Chapter 6, the best CIOs bridge the gap between the architects of the collaboration culture and the architect of the security culture, the CISO. These CIOs understand that collaboration and security must be mutually supportive for the goals of the organization to succeed. Without CIO-driven collaboration, achieving a competitive advantage is impossible. A CISO-driven security framework protects that collaborative culture and competitive advantage. A key part of the process in building an Insider Risk program involves measuring your level of maturity around Insider Risk management (IRM). To help accomplish that, we've built an IRM maturity framework tailored for the collaboration culture. We segmented the model based on three key areas:

1. People
2. Process
3. Technology

Across each of these components you indicate where you are in your maturity:

- Are you in the initial stages of your IRM journey?
- Do you outsource to a managed service provider?
- Have you defined all needed components of the IRM maturity framework?
- Do you have security and business metrics assigned and are you tracking them?
- And finally, are you analyzing performance to better optimize your IRM maturity?

Use the tables of variables on the following pages to evaluate your organization.

1	PEOPLE	Initial	Managed	Defined	Quantitatively Managed	Optimizing
1.1	IRM staff is accountable and program responsibilities are defined					
1.2	IRM program is staffed appropriately, commensurate to organizational risk					
1.3	Ongoing education and training are budgeted for IRM team					
1.4	Organizational awareness, support, and engagement are present at the executive level and among key internal stakeholders					
1.5	An environment of organizational IRM allies exists—e.g., the IRM program is appropriately transparent and engagement exists among company personnel (employees, contractors, vendors, etc.)					
1.6	Employee background checks are conducted commensurate to organizational/role risk and regulatory environment (considerations— previous employment, financial, criminal, social media, professional licensing, education, etc.)					

1	PEOPLE (continued)	Initial	Managed	Defined	Quantitatively Managed	Optimizing
1.7	New employees, contractors, and vendors receive appropriate training, expectations, and/or requirements that align with program goals and associated risks					
1.8	Relationships are established with external organizations for relevant and appropriate IRM intelligence and threat information—e.g., federal authorities, state law enforcement, professional organizations, or working groups as appropriate for your organization's industry and risk tolerance					

2	PROCESS	Initial	Managed	Defined	Quantitatively Managed	Optimizing
2.1	IRM program is documented, is commensurate with risk, and aligns with your organization's culture					
2.2	Key program elements are integrated into security policy and acceptable-use standards					
2.3	Insider risk elements are included in annual security training and awareness engagements					
2.4	IRM process accounts for the different risks of the employee life cycle—new hires, existing employees, transfers/promotions, performance improvement, departing employees, etc.					
2.5	IRM process integrates with relevant corporate processes—human resources, legal, procurement, vendor management, IT (devices, identity, and access life cycle management, application inventory, etc.)					
2.6	IRM program includes benchmarking and knowledge sharing with other companies					
2.7	Periodic Insider Risk and threat assessments, and program enhancements are conducted as needed					

3	TECHNOLOGY	Initial	Managed	Defined	Quantitatively Managed	Optimizing
3.1	Insider Risk tools that allow for monitoring and detection of user behavior and file exfiltration events and support investigation and response without stifling employee collaboration or productivity are implemented					
3.2	Insider Risk tools that provide monitoring and alerting capabilities across user end points, devices, web browsers, and cloud services are deployed					
3.3	Insider Risk management tools that integrate with workforce management, human resources, and IT ticketing systems are considered					
3.4	Tools that complement and enhance monitoring and alerting capabilities in your security technology stack are implemented					
3.5	Tools and technology that require low resource overhead (people, time, and budget) to maintain and run effectively are selected					
3.6	Tools that effectively scale with organizational growth, risk environment, and culture are implemented					

Section 3: Insider Risk Awareness Frameworks

Four Keys to Building a Security Awareness Program

1: Create a Clear Vision

Building a collaborative security-awareness program requires broad organizational buy-in. To move the needle toward that goal, communication and training are key. Security awareness messaging and training that focuses on consistent repetition, aligns with organizational core values, and engages employees is more likely to succeed.

Similar to advertising, employees need to hear a message multiple times and in multiple formats before they will notice and remember it. Share key messages in all channels where employees go for information, including employer chat forums such as Slack, email, audio, video, and written intranet content. Utilize security ambassadors to reinforce those messages. Ensure that language and images used in messaging and training are consistent with the organization's culture and core values and its vision of the future. Finally, make security awareness training and resources as easy, digestible, and brief as possible. Workers can easily fit a three- to seven-minute video training into their schedules on almost any given day, whereas they have to block their calendar for a thirty-minute training. When pointing employees toward resources, make sure they are easy to find. If you've got a data security policy, don't hide it behind a firewall that requires employees to use a VPN to access it. If outbound emails require encryption, place the instructions and tools in an easily accessible location.

2: Listen, Listen, Listen

To align an organization's security culture with its larger corporate culture, it's critical to understand your workers and what makes them tick. Listening is one of the most important qualities of a security leader and a security team. That involves getting out of the security office and engaging in open-ended listening. In a traditional face-to-face office environment, coffee chats with small groups are a great method to get to know people better. In a remote environment, leverage tools, such as Slack or Microsoft Teams, to join popular channels to find out what's on employees' minds. For organizations that rely more on voice than video calls, consider transitioning to video calls as a way to monitor whether team members are receiving the security-awareness messages the organization is trying to deliver. Video allows greater insight into facial expressions and micro expressions, which can facilitate more effective communication and the opportunity to adjust messaging if necessary.

3: Offer Positive Feedback

Providing positive feedback is one of the most effective ways to encourage compliance with Insider Risk programs. At Code42, even when we get above-average results from our phishing tests, we ask employees to go the extra mile in protecting the company. That's because even one successful phishing message can endanger organizational intellectual property. When they ace the tests, we take time to thank them. Gifts like gift cards, donuts, and pizza are always appreciated. Since those may not be easy to distribute in a remote environment, a heartfelt thank-you via email or on an all-company channel fuels the fire for everyone to continue to work together to keep protecting the company. Direct notes or recognition from the CISO or CEO are highly impactful in these situations.

4: Empower Everyone

The people who work for your organization are smart and driven or they wouldn't have been hired. That's why it's important to communicate with and train them for success, and empower them to protect the organization they contribute to every day. This effort should start at the top, with the c-suite establishing security awareness as an organizational priority. Security awareness training that is focused on establishing clear expectations around storing, sharing, or moving data is much more effective than training focused on spying on and reporting on coworkers. Because most security events and incidents are based on human error or negligence rather than malicious intention, an emphasis on assuming positive intent goes a long way toward establishing a favorable mindset toward security training.

Example: Code42 Security Ninja Program

As a security vendor, Code42 requires all employees to act and think like security professionals. Code42's Security Ninja Program is designed to cultivate company-wide security expertise. Through actively pursuing training and demonstrating appropriate security behavior, Security Ninjas help secure our collaborative culture. In return, the company celebrates this group of contributors with recognition, badges, and social media posts. The Security Ninja Program reinforces security-awareness training that we conduct as part of employee onboarding.

Security Ninja Belt	Goal: Increase Insider Risk knowledge and security expertise to better secure the collaboration culture, connect with the security buyer, and engage actively in the security ecosystem.
WHITE BELT	Successful completion of **two hours** of Insider Risk and cybersecurity curriculum and activities (above and beyond required security compliance training) covering topics such as: • Protecting data from Insider Risk • Building an Insider Risk program • Understanding personal mobile device guidelines • Understanding key security terms • Avoiding a phishing attack • Flagging and reporting phishing
YELLOW BELT Prerequisite: Security Ninja White Belt	Successful completion of **four hours** of Insider Risk and cybersecurity curriculum and activities (above and beyond required security compliance training) covering topics such as: • Data risk-exposure overview • Departing-employee data risk • How employees get hacked and what to avoid • Black hats vs. white hats • Cryptography basics • How to encrypt email communications • CISO recommended reading
GREEN BELT Prerequisite: Security Ninja Yellow Belt	Successful completion of **seven hours** of Insider Risk and cybersecurity curriculum and activities (above and beyond required security compliance training) covering topics such as: • Remote workforce data risk • Insider Risk market landscape • Insider Risk security challenges • Red Teams vs. Blue Teams • Red Team assignment • Security roundtable participation
BROWN BELT Prerequisite: Security Ninja Green Belt	Successful completion of **eight hours** of Insider Risk and cybersecurity curriculum and activities (above and beyond required security compliance training) covering topics such as: • Insider Risk prevention, detection, investigation, and response best practices • Internally sharing insider threat concepts with colleagues • Cloud security considerations for government and the military • Programming foundations: secure coding
BLACK BELT Prerequisite: Security Ninja Brown Belt	Successful completion of **fourteen hours** of Insider Risk and cybersecurity training (above and beyond required security compliance training) including: • Publishing an Insider Risk article • Delivering an Insider Risk presentation • Completing CISSP coursework

Section 4: Insider Risk Response Frameworks

Departing employees are one of the most common data exfiltration scenarios. When an organization believes that a departing or ex-employee has removed company information, there are a number of steps that can be taken to protect the organization. Demand letters sent to departing and ex-employees—and potentially to the new employer of the ex-employee—have the potential to safeguard the organization. These letters typically ask the departing or ex-employee to return or delete the information that they took. The demand letters also ask that the departing or ex-employee certify that the information was destroyed.

However, in some cases, sending such letters isn't appropriate. Factors to consider include:

- The specific information taken
- The circumstances under which the information was removed
- The amount of time that has elapsed since the information was taken
- The potential impact of the use of the information
- The industry of the ex-employee's current employer
- The likely response to the demand letter

We'll review these factors one by one.

What Information Did the Employee Take?

Not all information is significant enough to warrant a demand letter or next-employer notification. However, failure to pursue protection for trade secrets may jeopardize claims of trade secret status, and disclosure of confidential information may irreparably harm the organization.

Under What Circumstances Was the Information Taken?

Information taken under unusual circumstances may indicate that the ex-employee knew that taking the information violated the employee's obligations and intends to use the information. For example:

- Wiping the device after information is taken
- Deleting individual files after files are taken
- Renaming files with innocuous names before taking them
- Renaming files with a file type that does not match the actual file (e.g., a file named with a .jpg extension indicating that it is an image is actually a .xlsx spreadsheet file)
- Taking information outside normal working hours

How Much Time Has Elapsed Since the Information Was Taken?

With limited exceptions, the value of business information generally decreases with time. If a significant amount of time has elapsed since the ex-employee took the information, the current value of the information may not warrant a demand letter.

What Is the Impact If Employee Uses or Discloses the Information?

An ex-employee's use or disclosure of company information may result in a range of consequences. Evaluating the likelihood and severity of these consequences will inform the appropriate response. Questions to think about include:

- Would use or disclosure of the information result in competitive harm to the company?
- Would disclosure of the information create public relations concerns?
- Could the information be used to facilitate insider trading?
- Does the information include Personal Health Information (PHI) requiring regulatory reporting?
- Does the information include personal information that would trigger state data-breach notification requirements?
- Does the information include financial or payment information?
- Does the information include the confidential information of third parties, which may require reporting or result in a breach of contractual obligations?

What Is the Likely Response to a Demand Letter?

Ex-employees may react to a demand letter in a number of ways. In the ideal case, the ex-employee will return or delete any information taken and provide an attestation. But consider the impact if the ex-employee publishes the letter on social media or provides it to current employees. The perception of a company pursuing an ex-employee for immaterial violations of an employment agreement may impact current employees, prospects, and the company's reputation. Also consider how the company will react if the ex-employee ignores the letter and does not respond at all.

Insider Risk Response: Unauthorized Data Transfer

Dear [Employee Name]:

Our data and intellectual property are critical to our business, and we take data protection seriously. Your employee agreement and our corporate policies require you to protect the confidentiality of company data. As a reminder, you may only use company data to perform your job duties and only on company-approved devices and systems. We observed the transfer of company data in violation of company policies, the details of which are provided on Exhibit A. Please review and promptly delete all company data from the unauthorized device or system.

If you have any questions regarding this matter or whether a device or system is approved for company data, please contact the security department.

Sincerely,

Insider Risk Response: Unauthorized Data Transfer; Deletion Confirmation

Dear [Employee Name]:

Our data and intellectual property are critical to our business, and we take data protection seriously. Your employee agreement and our corporate policies require you to protect the confidentiality of company data. As a reminder, you may only use company data to perform your job duties and only on company-approved devices and systems. We observed the transfer of company data in violation of company policies, the details of which are provided on Exhibit A. Please review and promptly delete all company data from the unauthorized device or system. Email the Security Team at [_____] to confirm that you have permanently deleted the data.

If you have any questions regarding this matter or whether a device or system is approved for company data, please contact the security department.

Sincerely,

Insider Risk Response: Unauthorized Data Transfer and Deletion Attestation

Dear [Employee Name]:

Our data and intellectual property are critical to our business, and we take data protection very seriously. You signed an employee agreement with the company and agreed to abide by our corporate policies. Both of these require you to protect the confidentiality of data belonging to the company. You may only use company data to perform your job duties and only on company-approved devices and systems. We observed a transfer of company data in violation of your agreement and company policies ("Transfer"), the details of which are provided on Exhibit A.

Due to the seriousness of this matter, we require that you agree and acknowledge that:

- You have permanently deleted all company data involved in the Transfer (including any copies, duplicates, subsets, extracts, derivates, and related materials) from all unauthorized devices and systems.
- You have not transferred any other company data to unauthorized devices or systems.
- You have not allowed access to company data by an unauthorized third party.
- You have reviewed and acknowledged the applicable corporate policies and understand your responsibilities with regard to company data.
- [Any further unauthorized transfers may result in disciplinary action, including termination.]

If you have any questions regarding this matter or whether a device or system is approved for company data, please contact the security department.

By signing below, I confirm that I understand and agree to the above statements.

By: _____

Name: _____

Date: _____

Section 5: Building an Insider Risk Team

In Chapter 6, we talked about how the CISO empowers the security foundation of a collaborative culture. When a CISO is backed by a trusted team, security is much more effective and laser focused on the overall mission of the organization. Below is a template for what to look for when you are hiring an Insider Risk team member.

Insider Risk Analyst: Job Description

Responsibilities:

- Maintaining and updating insider threat risk-management policies and procedures
- Performing insider threat monitoring and alert management
- Conducting insider threat investigations in line with corporate culture and risk-management principles
- Performing insider threat case management and reporting
- Driving automation, process, and system integration into the insider threat management process
- Maintaining partnerships with key stakeholder teams, including legal and people teams
- Delivering and validating cloud and project security requirements
- Driving automation and efficiency into security processes, including consulting, third-party security, compliance, and security sales support
- Providing analysis and support for external audits and compliance initiatives, covering a range of information security frameworks that include but are not limited to NIST, SOC2, FedRAMP, ISO, and PCI-DSS
- Articulating the organization's security posture to customers and prospects
- Supporting the insider threat program
- Partnering with the sales team by supporting customer/prospect security due diligence efforts, including formal and ad hoc

security inquiries as well as customer security meetings
- Executing third-party security assessments of new and existing vendors
- Documenting security findings and risks, as well as recommendations for remediation
- Assisting with building and maintaining state of the art security program
- All other duties as assigned

Skills and requirements:

- Collaborative team player across the organization
- Bachelor's degree in relevant discipline
- Five or more years of experience in information security, compliance, and risk management
- Strong analytic and critical thinking abilities
- In-depth knowledge of audit processes and a variety of security frameworks
- Excellent verbal and written communication skills
- Strong understanding of security controls, frameworks, and practices

We will be especially impressed if you have experience in:

- SecDevOps
- Security tools and penetration testing
- NIST and FISMA federal security standards
- Coding

CHAPTER 10

The Collaboration Culture— Today and Tomorrow

Relying solely on security technology designed for an on-premises world to protect your now off-premises data simply isn't sustainable.
—Mark Wojtasiak, Vice President of Portfolio Strategy and Product Marketing, Code42

When we decided to write this book, we couldn't have imagined the extent to which a global pandemic would fast-forward the collaboration culture and magnify Insider Risk. Our team sat down to start the book on March 4, 2020, when the United States reported 158 total Covid-19 cases.[131] As we gathered in a conference room at our Minneapolis headquarters, we predicted that we'd all be working from home in short order.

We were right. Later in March, into the summer, and beyond, as many as 75 percent of office workers in the United States were sent home to work.[132] The pandemic moved the needle on remote work in a way that wouldn't have seemed possible before 2020. Think you can't get work done remotely? Don't fret—there's an app for that. Tools like Zoom, Slack, Microsoft Teams, G Suite, Google Drive, Microsoft OneDrive, HubSpot, Basecamp, Evernote, Microsoft OneNote, and more revolutionized cloud-based collaboration.

Yes, these tools existed pre-pandemic. However, the pandemic pushed the boundaries on productivity and collaboration, unleashing the workforce to create and innovate in the cloud. With millions of knowledge workers moving out from under the cybersecurity umbrella of their corporate offices, organizations lost visibility into their intellectual property and proprietary information. Everything from product road maps to source code, customer lists to sales forecasts, market research to financial results—it all went home with employees. For most organizations, once the data left the network it became invisible and, as a result, became a data security risk of immense proportion.

Relying solely on security technology designed for an on-premises world to protect your now off-premises data simply isn't sustainable. Security leaders, together with IT, legal, HR, and business partners, must move swiftly to secure a digital workforce now living in the cloud. Here's the challenge: Do it without ever compromising the speed of innovation or the safety of data.

In this final chapter, we'll showcase Ten Collaboration Culture Commandments inspired by this book. You can use them as a high-level road map for diagnosing and treating Insider Risk issues that stem from digital transformation and the collaboration culture. Then, we'll share ten predictions on the future of work, collaboration, and Insider Risk.

The Ten Collaboration Culture Commandments

Commandment #1: Find your aha moments and your data loss vulnerabilities

Data loss represents a major blind side for organizations of all sizes.

In their rush for time to market, time to revenue, and a competitive edge, organizations have found themselves more vulnerable to data loss than ever before. The potential for data to leak has never been greater, because exfiltrating it has never been easier. The consequences range from a contractor ripping off product designs to share with a competitor, to the very future viability of the organization.

Commandment #2: Make closing your data exfiltration gaps a priority

The monopoly on threat no longer belongs to those outside the virtual walls of your organization. It's inside, embedded in the very people, technology, and data that fuel it.

It's past time to acknowledge that the evolution in people, technology, and data that has created the collaboration culture has also created gaps in traditional data security systems. Organizations can't thrive without collaboration—the opportunity cost is too high. At the same time, they can't afford to let data exfiltration risk run wild in their organizations. Embracing collaboration means taking proactive steps to manage the Insider Risks that come with it.

Commandment #3: Accept that risk is risk regardless of intention—good, bad, or indifferent

Most employees are well-intentioned, but that doesn't mean well-intentioned behaviors do not cause risk.

Insider Risk cannot be viewed in absolute terms. There are shades of gray. We cannot assume that an employee taking data is doing so maliciously. At the same time, we cannot naively assume we don't have employees intending to harm the organization. Technology has made it easy for employees to work anytime, from anywhere—a reality that opens up companies to even more risk. As workers in this scenario, we all personally present some level of Insider Risk.

Commandment #4: Admit classification and blocking runs counter to a collaborative culture

The old conventional ways of protecting data are no longer enough to secure today's fast-paced collaborative cultures.

We can't ignore the simple fact that the very nature of blocking and forcing users to classify their data runs counter to the digitally powered cultures that are being built for collaborating and sharing. Relying solely on classification and blocking technology leaves organizations increasingly vulnerable to Insider Risk.

Commandment #5: Admit you're flying blind to the Insider Risks of cloud-based collaboration

If you currently lack visibility into the movement of data throughout your organization, you're vulnerable.

Organizations must realize that while digital transformation enables data access and collaboration, it also exposes the organization to Insider Risk. It's a direct trade-off—the more collaboration and access you give employees, the more opportunities they have to leak data outside the organization. It's impossible to seize all of the benefits of collaboration without the ramifications of Insider Risk.

Commandment #6: Empower CISOs to be digital enablers

To effectively secure the collaborative culture, the CISO must step into the leadership void and accept their role as powerful change agents.

For too long, the CISO has been viewed by the c-suite as a business blocker. As a result, the c-suite built the collaborative culture in the absence of the CISO. That forced the CISO to try to keep up with next-gen threats with last-gen tech. Today's progressive CISOs are embracing their roles as digital enablers. Their invaluable insider threat perspective should inform decisions throughout the organization. With insider threat rising, it's past time for the c-suite to offer the CISO a seat at the table.

Commandment #7: Don't rely on a non-compete to manage Insider Risk

If we are going to truly transform corporate culture to accommodate speed and collaboration, legal must adopt the same proactive stance demonstrated by the CISO, CIO, CHRO, CEO, and line-of-business leaders.

Non-compete agreements are yesterday's insider threat legal tools. Today's heightened Insider Risk environment requires strategic thinking from the general counsel and the entire legal team. Collaborating with the CISO, CHRO, and the CIO, the general counsel's task is to secure organizational intellectual property by going beyond the legal paper and aiding in Insider Risk detection and response.

Commandment #8: Invest in the employee experience

Strong collaboration cultures serve to deter Insider Risk.

You can't go wrong investing in the employee experience. Not only are employees more loyal to organizations offering a premium experience, those organizations also experience lower incidents of Insider Risk. That's because when employees are treated as trusted partners and informed as to the presence of Insider Risk programs, they are less likely to take data that doesn't belong to them. As the change agent in transforming the employee experience, the CHRO adds value through close collaboration with the CIO, CISO, and general counsel for the technology, security, and legal aspects of the employee experience.

Commandment #9: Build a sustainable Insider Risk framework

When it comes to building an Insider Risk program, there is no better place to start than the employee life cycle and the everyday events that trigger Insider Risk.

When it comes to managing or mitigating Insider Risk, you must take a more holistic programmatic approach. Insiders of all kinds put data at risk every day whether their intent is good, bad, or indifferent. In order to best manage and mitigate the every day risks, start by defining your own Insider Risk program. One that is rightsized for your organization.

Commandment #10: Invest in new tech

> *The solution to Insider Risk is technology that aims to understand how employees work, can distinguish between what is a threat and what is collaboration, and is easy to use so security teams can keep pace with the speed of the organization.*

Complexity is killing the security team's productivity. When exploring new tech, narrow your scope to SaaS-based solutions that are easy to deploy, manage, and use. Set clear buying requirements around mitigating file exposure and exfiltration risks without disrupting user productivity—and that goes for the security users as well. Finally, look for solutions that provide both company-wide and user-based visibility to Insider Risks. We all work at Code42. We are proud of the tech we have built because it strikes the balance between allowing collaboration and securing your data from exfiltration.

Where Do We Go from Here?

Now that you've absorbed these lessons, it's time to move forward, to the future. We don't have a crystal ball. But we've got experience and some insights into where the collaboration culture and inherent Insider Risks are headed.

Our Ten Future-of-Work Predictions

Prediction #1: The rise of the data risk intelligence platform

Organizations are awash in data—and that won't change anytime soon. What is changing are the types of data they collect and the motivations behind those activities. Monitoring takes various forms, including keystroke monitoring, tracking internal communications, and surveilling work devices. While this might seem creepy, organizations are quickly moving forward to add other forms of monitoring. The goal? Architect a data risk intelligence platform. As workforces become more distributed, organizations are going to increase efforts to track what's happening with data on and off the corporate network. Enhanced tracking of data, when done appropriately, provides organizations the data risk intelligence they need to manage and mitigate Insider Risk.

Prediction #2: Data loss prevention will be replaced by Insider Risk detection and response

There will be an evolution in the technology platforms that deal with insider threat and cybersecurity risks. As we've discussed in this book, we can't—and don't want to—turn back the clock. Organizations are only going to get more collaborative, more decentralized, and more fragmented. That translates into rising levels of Insider Risk. Over the course of the first nine chapters in this book, we've presented reams of credible evidence that digital transformation, collaborative cultures, and Insider Risk are highly correlated. To dodge the Insider Risk bullet means leveraging the best available resources to protect your organization today and tomorrow.

Prediction #3: Data security at the speed of 5G

Technology offers the chance to unleash digital transformation across the globe. A 5G network will connect people and their workplaces more efficiently, create smarter cities, speed transportation, and unleash an unprecedented wave of data. Lightning speed characterizes 5G, offering the potential to increase data-processing capacities by seven times. Organizations that can quickly leverage 5G for change can outpace their competitors much in the same way that the technology companies that grew out of the 2008–2009 financial crisis came to dominate their sectors.[133] Of the many changes that 5G will bring, improvements in automation, AI, and machine learning promise some of the biggest benefits while the speed at which we work literally anywhere at any time on any device will ultimately present greater Insider Risk.

Prediction #4: Prioritization of well-being at work and at home

Most organizations that prioritize the employee experience don't sit still. They continually seek ways to improve that experience by analyzing what others are doing and listening to their employees. The employee experience will move closer to nirvana when employees feel completely at home at work and when that experience fully embraces the overall concept of well-being. While this was already a trend pre-Covid, the pandemic made it a reality as both employers and employees came to understand the importance of remote work in protecting employees from Covid-19 infections. As employers consider protocols for returning to work, holistic well-being programs should be high on their list. While remote work has protected employees from Covid-19, it's exposed them to burnout from working too much, and caretaking for children and other relatives.

Prediction #5: Workplaces become workspaces

The pandemic fast-forwarded remote work. Knowledge-based organizations and their employees rapidly shifted from complete office to complete remote work in days. Going forward, organizations have the opportunity to optimize an improved balance of office and remote work. Depending on employee preferences, job functions, organizational goals, and data, an ideal mix of remote and in-person work can capture the benefits of collaboration and flexibility. When done right, this new work reality can drastically improve the employee experience as well as organizational bottom lines.

Prediction #6: From crowdsourcing to cloud sourcing

For companies to thrive in the future means embracing an even faster-paced business model. Instead of waiting to get far-flung leaders together, organizations and ecosystems will utilize cloud technologies like never before to innovate faster in near real time. In a similar manner, product development talent will be leveraged across and among organizations—regardless of location—to cut the time to product, market, and value curves. Everything will go agile.

Prediction #7: Resiliency planning gets strategic

In the future of work, strategic planning will need to demonstrate even more flexibility. Neither the present nor the future is static. That means building adaptability and resiliency into strategic planning—creating a landscape of potential strategies rather than committing too much energy to any one forecast. That also means embracing a more radical vision of change. Because in a world filled with turmoil, incrementalism doesn't move the needle—bold, creative, and innovative change fuels success.

Prediction #8: Digital failure is not an option

Going forward, digital transformation will move faster and create a more sizable competitive advantage. It's easier than ever to get what you want with one click. That means organizations that deliver seamless experiences to their employees, customers, and stakeholders have an edge. However, this edge is fleeting because you can't get complacent as digital transformation continues to move at light speed. Organizations that continually reinvent and reinvent again position themselves for success.

Prediction #9: Reimagination of organizational footprints

Work can happen wherever and whenever it's most convenient and effective for people and their organizations. That means organizational leaders will need to be even bolder in determining what their future footprint looks like. Many organizations recognize a need for in-person interaction and connection at physical workplaces, while also honoring the needs of their employees for more work-life balance and a flexible work schedule. With that in mind, organizations will need to create more flexible blueprints for encouraging important interactions, while enhancing work-life balance. That could mean cutting centralized office space and adding smaller satellite office locations in more affordable areas. Or it could mean 100 percent remote work with consistent in-person interactions several times a year. The key is determining how to best align your organizational footprint with your objectives and employee experience.

Prediction #10: The rise of the chief change agents and risk officers

The organizations that thrive will include the top change agents in the c-suite—CEO, CISO, CIO, CHRO, general counsel—and a seat holder for the CRO (Chief Risk Officer). These change agents are responsible for both the organization's digital transformation and managing the risks that come with it. There will only be more opportunities for organizations to digitally disrupt. Like change, disruption is constant, and the chief change agents and risk officers will identify the best moments to enact that change. To accomplish needed change, it will be their role to prioritize the organization's top issues, build a vision for change, communicate the reasons for the change, and move toward that change with a collaborative and secure approach.

Acknowledgments

Books don't write themselves. There is a cast of folks we want to thank for not only capturing our vision for data security and Insider Risk in words, but also those who inspired that vision.

Thank you to our customers whose stories and insights are included in the pages of our book: BAYADA Home Health Care, a leading provider of in-home healthcare and support services; MacDonald-Miller, a full-service, design-build mechanical contractor in the Pacific Northwest; The Pokémon Company International, responsible for brand management, production, marketing and licensing of the Pokémon franchise; Shape Technologies Group, the world's leading supplier of waterjet technology and ultrahigh-pressure manufacturing process solutions; and the YMCA of the Greater Twin Cities, a nonprofit for youth development, healthy living, and social responsibility. And thanks to the hundreds of other customers whose ideas grace these pages, but who would prefer to remain unmentioned by name. You are all proof that securing the collaboration culture is not only possible, it's also essential to the future of business.

We are grateful for our industry partners, who are open to new ideas and challenging the holy grails of data security: Ron Gula, cyber industry pioneer, developer of Dragon, one of the first commercial network intrusion detection systems, and cofounder of Tenable Network Security; Chip Heath, author of best-sellers *Switch*, *Made to Stick*, *Decisive*, and *The Power of Moments*; George Kurtz, cofounder, president, and CEO of CrowdStrike; Martin Roesch, cybersecurity expert, creator of Snort, and founder of Sourcefire; David Meerman Scott, marketing strategist, entrepreneur and best-selling author of eleven books, including *Fanocracy* and *The New Rules of Marketing & PR*; Dug Song, cybersecurity expert, cofounder and CEO of Duo Security, and cofounder of Arbor Networks; and Amit Yoran, CEO of Tenable, former president of RSA, former national cybersecurity director at DHS, and former director of US-CERT.

Thank you to Amy Buttell for the time you spent getting to know Code42 and the many hours that went into making our book a reality; and Amanda Ayers Barnett for your help in the editing process.

Thank you to our colleagues at Code42: Alexandra Gobbi and Gerri Dyrek, who spent countless hours reading and reviewing and suggesting ideas for this book; and David Huberman and Leslie Pendergrast for your leadership and championing our collaborative culture.

We also want to thank all of the Guardians at Code42. What are Guardians? They are our employees. They are the five hundred talented people our customers rely on to safeguard their data every day. They are a true example of what it means to live out a collaboration culture—never compromising the speed of innovation for the safety of data. Thank you for bringing your very best to Code42.

Endnotes

Chapter 1

1 "Culture Change," Code42 Sales Slide Library, March 20, 2020.

2 "Employee Turnover," Code42 Sales Slide Library, March 20, 2020.

3 "Insider Threat Report 2019," Verizon.

4 "Combating the Insider Threat," US National Cybersecurity and Communications Investigation Center, May 2, 2014.

5 "The Culture Gap," Code42 Sales Slide Library, March 20, 2020.

6 Brooke, Chris, "Ex-Worker Stole 'Crown Jewels' Before Leaving Company," *Data Insider*, January 28, 2020.

7 Albergotti, Reed, "Criminal prosecutors to drop trade secret charges against former Fitbit employees," *Washington Post*, February 14, 2020.

8 Canal, Emily, "Jawbone, Once Valued at $3 billion, Is Going Out of Business. Here's What Went Wrong," Inc.com, July 7, 2017.

9 Goode, Lauren, "Judge invalidates Fitbit patents in suit against Jawbone," TheVerge.com, July 20, 2020.

10 "Fitbit, Jawbone Announce Deal to End Sprawling IP War," Law360.com, December 14, 2017.

11 "The Culture Gap," Code42 Sales Slide Library, March 20, 2020.

[12] Code42 Data Exposure Report 2019.

[13] Dtex Systems, "New ESG Research Confirms Organizations Continue to Struggle with Insider Threat Detection," CISION PR Newswire, August 2, 2019.

[14] "Insider Threat Report 2019," Verizon.

[15] Vijayan, Jaikumar, "Update: SunPower lawsuit highlights insider threat," ComputerWorld.com, February 14, 2012.

[16] Dean, "Insider theft in the news again," digitalendpoint.com, March 13, 2015.

[17] Reuters, "SunPower sues former executive over trade secrets," Yahoo! Finance, June 21, 2019.

[18] Beets, Becky, "SunPower files lawsuit against SunEdison, former employees for poaching trade secrets," PVmagazine.com, June 4, 2015.

Chapter 2

[19] Zeinder, Rita, "Coronavirus Makes Work from Home the New Normal," SHRM.com, March 21, 2020.

[20] Hickman, Adam, Ph.D., and Lydia Saad, "Reviewing Remote Work in the U.S. Under COVID-19," Gallup.com, May 22, 2020.

[21] Costello, Katie, and Gloria Omale, "Gartner Predicts by 2021, CIOs Will Be as Responsible for Culture Change as Chief HR Officers," Gartner.com, February 11, 2019.

[22] "10,000 Baby Boomers Turn 65 Every Day," Transamerica, 2013.

[23] "By 2030, All Baby Boomers Will be 65 or Older," United States Census Bureau, December 10, 2019.

[24] Fry, Richard, "Millennials are the largest generation in the U.S. labor force," Pew Research Center, April 11, 2019.

[25] Bontas, Raluca, "Leading the social enterprise: Reinvent with a human focus," Deloitte.

26 Ibid.

27 "The Future of Work is Human: 2019 International Employee Survey Report," WorkHuman, September 3, 2019.

28 Ibid.

29 Ibid.

30 Chapman, Paul, "How CIOs can empower today's digital native workforce," CIO.com, March 27, 2018.

31 Leung, Iris, "Report: Only 7% of Workers Feel Productive During Work Hours," Forbes.com, August 31, 2017.

32 Maurer, Roy, "Flexible Work Critical to Retention, Survey Finds," SHRM.com, September 10, 2019.

33 Dvorak, Nate, and Rachael Breck, "Do you offer as much flexibility as you say you do?" Gallup.com, November 27, 2018.

34 Hess, Abigail, "The 20 best companies for work-life balance," CNBC.com, May 4, 2017.

35 Ludwig, Sean, "10 Forward-Looking Companies Offering Flexible Work," U.S. Chamber of Commerce, February 21, 2020.

36 Davis, Michelle, and Jeff Green, "Three Hours Longer, the Pandemic Workday Has Obliterated Work-Life Balance," Bloomberg.com, April 23, 2020.

37 Code42 Data Exposure Report 2020.

38 Hering, Beth Braccio, "Remote Work Statistics: Shifting Norms and Expectations," FlexJobs.com, February 13, 2020.

39 Schwab, Klaus, "The Fourth Industrial Revolution: What it means, how to respond," World Economic Forum, January 14, 2016.

40 Ibid.

41 Ibid.

42 "Centre for the Fourth Industrial Revolution," World Economic Forum.

[43] FPT-Software, "How Tesla Changed the Automotive Industry Forever," fpt-software.com, 2019.

[44] Levin, Tim, "All the things carmakers say they'll accomplish with their future electric vehicles between now and 2030," BusinessInsider.com, January 28, 2020.

[45] Code42 Data Exposure Report 2019.

Chapter 3

[46] Beets, Becky, "SunPower files lawsuit against SunEdison, former employees for poaching trade secrets," PVmagazine.com, June 4, 2015.

[47] Ibid.

[48] Overly, Steven, "U.S. charges Huawei with decades-long theft of U.S. trade secrets," Politico.com, February 13, 2020.

[49] Lahiri, Tripti, "The US says Huawei had a bonus program for employees who stole trade secrets," Quartz, January 29, 2019.

[50] Cimpanu, Catalin, "US charges Huawei with racketeering and conspiracy to steal trade secrets," ZDNet, February 13, 2020.

[51] Office of Public Affairs, "Chinese Telecommunications Conglomerate Huawei and Subsidiaries Charged in Racketeering Conspiracy and Conspiracy to Steal Trade Secrets," United States Department of Justice, February 13, 2020.

[52] Nellis, Stephen, "Ex-Apple worker charged with stealing self-driving car trade secrets," Reuters, July 10, 2018.

[53] Horwitz, Jeremy, "Ex-Apple employee charged with stealing autonomous vehicle secrets," VentureBeat, July 10, 2018.

[54] Stangel, Luke, "Ex-Apple employee pleads not guilty to stealing secret blueprints for self-driving car project," Silicon Valley Business Journal, July 17, 2018.

[55] Code42 Data Exposure Report 2019.

[56] McGrane, Clare, "Personal data of 36,000 Boeing employees put at risk after employee emails info to spouse," GeekWire.com, March 1, 2017.

[57] Muncaster, Phil, "Boeing Employee Exposes Colleagues' Data in Privacy Snafu," Infosecurity Group, February 27, 2017.

[58] KOMO Staff, "36,000 Boeing employees impacted by security breach after worker sent email to spouse," KomoNews, March 1, 2017.

[59] McIntosh, Andrew, "Boeing discloses 36,000-employee data breach after email to spouse for help," Puget Sound Business Journal, February 28, 2017, updated March 1, 2017.

[60] Campbell, Kerry, "1,041 P.E.I. dental patients identified in privacy breach," CBCnews.com, June 5, 2019.

[61] Ibid.

[62] Ibid.

[63] Ibid.

[64] Ibid.

[65] Ibid.

Chapter 4

[66] Chickowski, Erika, "6 Reasons Why Employees Violate Security Policies," Darkreading.com, October 16, 2018.

[67] "2020 Cost of Insider Threats Global Report," Ponemon, 2020.

[68] "Insider Threats Rise by 47% in Two Years: Report," CISOMag.com, April 28, 2020.

[69] Ibid.

[70] "Unemployment rate rises to record high 14.7 percent in April 2020," U.S. Bureau of Labor Statistics, May 13, 2020.

Chapter 5

[71] LinkedIn.com, "YMCA of the Greater Twin Cities."

[72] "Twin Cities Reports Largest Population Jump in Recent Years," CBS Minnesota, March 22, 2018.

[73] Costello, Katie, "Gartner Survey Reveals That CEO Priorities Are Slowly Shifting to Meet Rising Growth Challenges," Gartner.com, May 8, 2019.

[74] PwC 22nd Annual Global CEO Survey 2019.

[75] Ibid.

[76] Costello, Kate, and Gloria Omale, "Gartner Predicts by 2021, CIOs Will Be as Responsible for Culture Change as Chief HR Officers," Gartner. com, February 11, 2019.

[77] Ibid.

[78] Baker, Mary, "5 Imperatives for HR Leaders to Tackle the Future of Work," Gartner.com, October 28, 2019.

[79] Ibid.

[80] "CIOs Aren't Willing to Settle for Repackaged Consumer Technology," Coolfire, August 20, 2019.

[81] Code42 Data Exposure Report 2019.

[82] Ibid.

[83] Ibid.

[84] Ibid.

[85] Ibid.

[86] Ibid.

[87] Code42 Data Exposure Report 2019 and 2020.

[88] Ibid.

[89] Code42 Data Exposure Report 2019.

[90] Ibid.

[91] Ibid.

Chapter 6

[92] Beets, Becky, "SunPower files lawsuit against SunEdison, former employees for poaching trade secrets," PVmagazine.com, June 4, 2015.

[93] Reuters, "SunPower sues former executive over trade secrets," Yahoo! Finance, June 21, 2019.

[94] Zand, Joel, "SunPower Sues SolarCity and ex-Employees Over Trade Secrets, Alleging Theft of 'Tens-of-Thousands' of Files," Justia Law Blog, February 14, 2012.

[95] Groom, Nichola, "SunPower sues former executive over trade secrets," Reuters, June 21, 2019.

[96] "Insider Threat Report 2019," Verizon.

[97] Boyer, Stephen, "We're all at risk when 65% of stressed-out cybersecurity and IT workers are thinking about quitting, tech exec warns," CNBCNews.com, October 11, 2019.

Chapter 7

[98] "Non-Compete Contracts: Economic Effects and Policy Implications," Office of Economic Policy, U.S. Department of the Treasury, March 2016.

[99] Quinn, Gene, "What is a Confidentiality Agreement and Why are they So Important?" IPWatchdog.com, December 16, 2017.

[100] Martinez, Michael E., Sang-yul Lee, Lauren Norris Donahue, Erinn L. Rigney, Brian J. Smith, "Competition in U.S. Labor Markets: Non-Compete Clauses Increasingly Under Fire," National Law Review, January 27, 2020.

[101] Ibid.

[102] Flanagan, Jane, and Terri Gerstein, "Welcome Developments on Limiting Non-Compete Agreements," American Constitutional Society, November 7, 2019.

[103] "New Decade, New Resolve to Protect and Promote Competitive Markets for Workers," US Federal Trade Commissioner Office of Commissioner Rebecca Kelly Slaughter," January 9, 2020.

[104] "H.R. 5710–Workforce Mobility Act of 2020," Congress.gov, January 29, 2020.

[105] Katz, Debra, and Lisa Banks, "Bloomberg nondisclosure agreement controversy misses why victims can want them," NBCNews.com, February 22, 2020.

[106] Hong, Nicole, "End of the Nondisclosure Agreement? Not So Fast," *Wall Street Journal*, March 26, 2018.

[107] Smith, Michelle R., "Some states place limits on secret harassment settlements," AP.com, August 27, 2018.

[108] "California Consumer Privacy Act (CCPA)," OAG.CA.gov, June 1, 2020.

[109] Wolford, Ben, "What is GDPR, the EU's new data protection law?" Intersoft consulting.

[110] "Art. 17 GDPR, Right to erasure ('right to be forgotten')," Intersoft Consulting.

[111] Lataille, Nancie, and Gabriella Kilby, "The Legal Function Transformed: Best Practices of Today's General Counsel," Korn Ferry.

Chapter 8

[112] "Core beliefs and cultures," Deloitte.

[113] "State of Work 2020," Workfront.

[114] Harter, Jim, "4 Factors Driving Record-High Employee Engagement in U.S.," Gallup.com, February 4, 2020.

[115] Campbell, George, "The employee experience (EX) statistics you should know in 2020," Qualtrics, June 25, 2019.

[116] Hess, Abigail, "Workers quit their jobs at the fastest rate on record in 2019—here's why," CNBC.com, January 8, 2020.

[117] "Win with Empathy," Mercer, May 18, 2020.

[118] Dension, Dan, "Bringing Corporate Culture to the Bottom Line," *Organizational Dynamics* 13, no. 2 (February 1984): 4–22, DOI: 10.1016/0090-2616(84)90015-9.

[119] Harter, Jim, and Annamarie Mann, "The Right Culture: Not Just About Employee Satisfaction," Gallup.com, April 12, 2017.

[120] Ibid.

[121] Whitehouse, Tammy, "Where Culture Languishes, Fraud Risks Proliferate," *Wall Street Journal*, November 4, 2019.

[122] Ibid.

[123] Powers, Brian, "4 Strategies to Improve Collaboration Between Legal & HR," HR Technologist, November 21, 2019.

[124] Capelli, Peter, and Anna Tavis, "The Performance Management Revolution," *Harvard Business Review* (October 2016).

Chapter 9

[125] Office of Public Affairs, "Chinese Company Sinovel Wind Group Convicted of Theft of Trade Secrets," United States Department of Justice, January 24, 2018.

[126] Ibid.

[127] Ibid.

[128] Ibid.

[129] Burgess, Christopher, "Sinovel Wind Group found guilty of IP theft, fined $1.5 million," CSO.com, July 9, 2018.

[130] Ibid.

Chapter 10

[131] Hollingsworth, Julia, Adam Renton, Steve George, Emma Reynolds, Mike Hayes, Rachel Bowman and Meg Wagner, "March 4 coronavirus news," CNN.com, March 4, 2020.

[132] "When everyone can work from home, what's the office for?" PwC, June 25, 2020.

[133] "The 5G edge computing value opportunity," KPMG, June 2020.

Index

CODE42

Inside jobs require outside action.

Visit Code42.com to learn how our solution detects and responds to Insider Risk with signal, simplicity and speed.

Experience your own aha moment with a 30-day free trial: **Code42.com/trial**